Pastoral
Care with
Stepfamilies

Pastoral Care with Stepfamilies

Mapping the Wilderness

LOREN L. TOWNSEND

Chalice Press®
St. Louis, Missouri

Cover photography: Left – Adobe Image Library CD and Right – Picture Quest
Cover design: Bob Currie
Art direction: Michael A. Domínguez
Interior design: Wynn Younker

This book is printed on acid-free, recycled paper.

Visit Chalice Press on the World Wide Web at
www.chalicepress.com

10 9 8 7 6 5 4 3 2 1   00 01 02 03

Library of Congress Cataloging–in–Publication Data

Townsend, Loren L.
    Pastoral care with stepfamilies : mapping the wilderness / Loren L. Townsend.
        p.   cm.
    ISBN 0-8272-2966-6
    1. Church work with stepfamilies   I. Title.
    BV4439.5 .T69   2000
    259' .1—dc21
                                                        00–009141

CONTENTS

PREFACE

Last year I was invited to speak to a church evangelism committee about how the church can reach stepfamilies. During the consultation, I noticed an odd, recurrent pattern of speech. Every reference to stepfamilies was articulated in nouns and verbs that placed them outside the church and beyond the usual reach of ministry. "They" were "out there." "They" were strangers by whom congregational leaders and pastors were confused and disoriented. Oddly, when I asked if the church had among its membership any divorced and remarried people, I was quickly told about several families that had come to the staff's attention amid a church of hundreds. Because of the pastoral care problems they presented, they were known to be stepfamilies. The staff acknowledged that they had little sense about how to respond to these families, and they could point to few positive outcomes of their intervention. Clearly, the divorced and remarried families to whom they referred were the "other" who did not fit easily into congregational life or usual pastoral care strategies. After considerable thought, the church staff remembered two church leaders who each had long ago been divorced and remarried. However, since each of them appeared to have an effective family life, the staff had never really considered either of their families as stepfamilies.

In fact, the ministry team with which I consulted was partly right. Stepfamilies *are* mostly "out there." They are separated from full inclusion in the life of the church even when they are members of a congregation. Divorced and remarried families are *different* from traditional families we have come to know and with whom we have learned to minister. Their internal and intergenerational processes are different, and their needs are different. Successful stepfamilies look different than successful nuclear families. These pastors had a right to be confused.

Because of changes in family demographics over the past 30 years, congregations must now take stepfamilies seriously. They are with us and are important members of the body of Christ. They have a significant contribution to make to our understanding of the image of God in humanity. They have gifts for the ministry and mission of the church, and they need care. Most important, they are no longer "they"; they are "us." It is the task of the church at the turn of the millennium to make theological sense of stepfamily life and, out of this understanding, begin to build systems of care that can respond to stepfamily reality.

The stepfamily pilgrimage leads through wild and unknown territory. Often there are no companions, no maps, and no reliable compass. Clouds dim any sense of direction from guiding stars or faithful sun. To live in a stepfamily requires improvisation, creativity, and the fortitude to start over when the illusion of a path ends at a rocky cliff. A wilderness provides unknown challenges. Today's survival may require picking carefully through dense brush to arrive safely at a small clearing promising some rest. Tomorrow's journey may require desert survival along a path littered with the desiccated remains of past travelers, which shatter all hope of finding water or shade. Other days, the beauty of the wilderness is beyond compare and "challenge" is meaningless.

Stepfamilies live in a wilderness land. They must learn to survive and orient when the landscape is unfamiliar. They must learn to build homes where they are strangers and aliens. Ministry with stepfamilies is a corresponding wilderness trek. Familiar tools of family ministry break when used in this uncultivated land; old or intuitive maps fail to show the land's contours accurately. Compasses are pulled off-course by emotional fields distorting a sense of direction. Yet the church's directive is ministry to the homeless and to those whose hope has failed.

Ministry with stepfamilies begins in companionship on this wilderness journey. There is no sure path. There is no sure end. There is only God's promised presence. "Never curse your wilderness" stated an African American minister in a pastoral-counseling seminar. It is a place of burning bushes and water that springs from rocks. It's a place where demons show their hands and temptations glow in raw appeal. Wilderness is a place of formation that pits hope against despair and God's promise against annihilation. It's a place where unexpected companions suddenly appear, where angels sustain those who faint, and the quiet voice of God is heard. Hope and a theological identity are formed in a wilderness where no map can guide, no well-used trails appear, and no guiding star points the way.

This book assumes that God has called congregations and caring ministers to accompany stepfamilies into wilderness. It is written to pastors, pastoral care specialists, church leaders, and seminary students, and claims a threefold agenda. My first purpose is to highlight and outline primary themes in American culture and stepfamily life that characterize how divorced and remarried families depart from expected nuclear family norms. We must understand this "differentness," or "otherness," if we are to begin any theological interpretation of stepfamilies that can guide pastoral care. Chapters 1 and 2 describe the religious and social location of stepfamilies in a culture dominated by nuclear family norms. Chapters 4 through 7 identify core stepfamily experiences and are meant to help the reader attend carefully to stepfamily voices. Careful listening anchors twin theological tasks: interpreting with stepfamilies their place in the community of faith and providing congregational care.

A second purpose of this book is to describe a model of reflective care that grounds companionship with stepfamilies. The method I propose in chapter 3 begins in stepfamily experience and insists that the church itself be affected by stepfamily stories in a way that demands interpretation, theological discovery, and creative pastoral care. This method attends to individual families, but also calls the church to prophetic advocacy against those social, cultural, and religious powers that disenfranchise and subjugate stepfamily hope.

This text is not intended to be a hopeful, helpful, how-to manual for pastors who want to apply ready-made solutions to their "stepfamily problem" or problem stepfamilies. Neither is it an authoritative last word about what stepfamilies need or what specific actions a church should take with remarried families. Stepfamilies are far too diverse for a "cookbook" approach to pastoral care. Congregational cultures vary so widely that recipes are of little value. Instead, congregations must learn to listen to the depth of stepfamily stories and engage them toward wholeness and restoration.

In these chapters I hope to articulate the cutting edge of stepfamily hope and pain. Using a speculative case study in chapter 8, I also hope to demonstrate a method that roots congregational care in the constructive theological imagination of individual congregations and the whole community of faith. In this process, the church's understanding of God grows, and its mission is refined. At the same time, stepfamilies are engaged in their unique strengths and needs rather than treated like recycled nuclear families, with whom we are more familiar.

Stepfamilies are with us and will continue to be with us. They are us. Including stepfamilies fully in the life of the church requires a theological interpretation of divorced and remarried families and a moral vision for stepfamily life. My final agenda for this book is experimental and propositional. If we bring stepfamily experience into constructive dialogue with the church and its faith resources, what might the result of this theological and mutually informative task look like? Chapter 9 draws together four inchoate dialogical themes around which constructive theological discourse can organize. This conversation is the task immediately in front of a church concerned with caring for stepfamilies and facilitating their full participation in the body of Christ. In the last analysis, this work is intended to be one that names the reality of stepfamily life and then points to hope manifested in the community of Christ.

As a pastor, theologian, pastoral counselor, divorced person, husband, father, and stepfather, I am unable to approach any pastoral consideration of stepfamilies with anything less than passion. I have lived a stepfamily life for many years and have experienced firsthand its pain, joy, success, and failure. It is not only "they" who are marginalized by public policy, social climate, and religious prejudice, it is also me and mine. To live in a stepfamily is to live on uncertain cultural ground, whether it be as an American subject to unpredictable judicial processes or as a church member whose family at times bears the blame for a variety of ills and then fits neatly into the blind spots of a congregation's nuclear family vision. To tell parts of the stepfamily story in this book is also to share fragments of my own, my children's, and my stepchildren's story. Consequently, an element of passion is unavoidable. I would want it no other way.

This book was made possible by many people. I first want to express my thanks to Louisville Presbyterian Theological Seminary and its board of directors, who supported my research and granted me sabbatical leave to complete this work. Countless clients and workshop participants confidentially provided words, ideas, and the raw experience of stepfamily life. I owe them a debt of gratitude for their anonymous voices and stories. Without the privilege of their trust and their courage to share, I would have few words but my own.

Becky Timerding, administrative assistant for Louisville Seminary's Marriage and Family Therapy Program, deserves special praise for her contribution to this book. Without her sentinel spirit posted daily at my office door, the monotonous rhythms of office life would have spirited away all creative inspiration. To my colleagues who gave their time in conversation and in reading unrefined manuscript pages (Leslie Smith Kendrick, John McClure, and Brad Wigger) and to those who gave the gift of encouragement (Nancy Ramsay, Larry Graham, Gene March, and Diane Reistroffer), I also offer my deep thanks.

Finally, I want to offer special thanks to my children, Nathan and Leslea, who have shared a journey with me and have taught me more about stepfamily life than I ever wanted to know. They are testimonies to faithfulness, resilience, and God's gift of hope. I want to express my gratitude to my wife and colleague Leslie Smith Kendrick and my stepdaughters, Sarah and Chelsea, who continue to teach me how to be a stepfather.

PART ONE
Foundations

Chapter 1

A Glimpse of the Landscape

A Stepfamily's Story

Ron and Julie Brown joined their suburban church soon after marrying two years ago. They wanted to start their marriage in a congregation they had chosen together. This was a second marriage for both, and they wanted things to go well. Ron had been divorced for two years and Julie for four when the couple married. Ron has two children from his first marriage—a daughter, thirteen, and a son, ten. His children spend every other weekend, alternating holidays, and some summer vacation with him. Those who know Ron have heard his story of an expensive, bloody divorce and the abusive child support payments he makes monthly to an undeserving ex-wife. Ron was not able to recover financially in the two years between divorce and remarriage, and brought significant debt into his new relationship.

Julie has three children from her previous marriage—two sons, fifteen and nine, and one daughter, age seven. Only those closest to her know that she was first married at eighteen. For twelve years she was a homemaker in a traditional marriage that ended suddenly when her husband left her for a younger woman. Julie doesn't like to talk about losing her home or about her poverty after the divorce. She is embarrassed about how she had to live for four years as a single parent. She is unable to collect her court-ordered child support, but she is not legally allowed to deny her husband his rights to visitation. She knows Ron resents this.

Pastor Smith first saw Ron and Julie as typical newlyweds. The couple lived with some tension, but they were also filled with hope. They seemed to be a model blended family. Like many new church members with strong religious backgrounds, the couple had shown promise as leaders. But over the last two years, they had become ambivalent about church commitments. Given the pressure of dual working schedules and school activities, the pastoral staff did not find this unusual.

During lunch one day, pastor Smith met Julie at a local deli. Tearfully, Julie told pastor Smith that she and Ron were in the final stages of divorce. In a story punctuated by anger and sorrow, Julie told of shattered dreams, the illusion of a second chance, and the pain she and Ron had endured over the last two years. She was angry with her pastors and church. Not only was the church unsupportive, but she felt the church had actively discouraged her stepfamily from becoming involved. Lack of a supportive religious community, she felt, had contributed to her family's failure. Pastor Smith was shocked by Julie's disclosure and left the encounter confused, angry, and hurt.

At the next staff meeting, Pastor Smith told her colleagues about her conversation. After much discussion, the group concluded that they had done everything possible to treat the Browns like any other family. They had not been excluded, nor had the church acted with discrimination. Ron and Julie had rarely attended programs meant to support church families. How did they expect to benefit if they did not attend? The staff concluded that had the couple been more forthcoming with their pain, they might have been referred to a pastoral counselor for family therapy. Instead, they hid their pain and had not made themselves available for help. Now pastors and church members were targets for Julie's anger and grief.

In follow-up visits, pastor Smith listened as Julie and Ron talked about their experience. She heard several themes. First, stepfamily living was difficult and often painful. Both felt it remarkable that their problems had been "invisible" to church leadership. Why had no one asked about Rob's thirteen-year-old daughter when she acted out in Sunday school? No one seemed to care that Julie's nine-year-old son was repeating third grade or that Ron and Julie were rarely together at church gatherings. Ron mused at one point that their family was so second-class that God hadn't even bothered to provide help. Even the marriage and parenting programs offered by the church offered little for their stepfamily. When they followed the advice given by speakers and family-life literature, their problems usually increased. Where was the Christian promise of redemption and renewal for divorced and remarried families? He could not recall ever hearing a sermon or Sunday school lesson about this.

Julie was particularly angry about her children. What guidance was there from the church? How were they supposed to live out so-called Christian parenting when their children lived in two separate homes and were accountable to four parents? Where was God's presence in the loyalty conflicts that were so real to their life and with their children? What images of God's grace were their children going to internalize?

In different conversations, Ron and Julie told pastor Smith how excluded they felt in regular church activities. Their children were not chosen for parts in plays and musical productions because visitation schedules resulted in unpredictable attendance. Likewise, their names were often left off play or musical programs when they did participate. This was explained, of course, by the fact that leaders were not certain they were truly taking part. Ultimately, the children felt they had no friends and no connection with the church. They did not want to attend. Ron and Julie felt unsupported in providing religious education and a spiritual foundation for their children.

Pastor Smith listened as Ron talked about his isolation. As a couple, he and Julie were never able to build close relationships with people in whom they could confide. Part of the problem was time. Ron worked excessively to support a complex family budget and to manage visitation schedules. However, church programs themselves seemed designed to undergird the needs of families made up of of first-married couples and their children. It was hard to talk about their experience as a couple who had been divorced and remarried. It was hard to share the complex feelings about living with children biologically related to one parent, but not to the other. No one, it seemed, understood their stress as they tried to nurture a marriage with no time alone. No one noticed how they tried to hold a new family together in very trying circumstances. Or no one chose to respond.

By the end of several visits, pastor Smith began to wonder about ministry to stepfamilies. Was the church somehow missing the needs of these nontraditional families? Could this relate to the declining church membership that so concerned her staff and denomination?

Stepfamilies and Contemporary Life

Voltaire once quipped that divorce was invented about the same time as marriage—about two weeks later, to be exact. In some form, divorce has existed in all human cultures. However, American social patterns centralize divorce in an uncommon way. It is imbedded so deeply in the laws, institutions, manners, and mores of contemporary American life that social critics have labeled ours a "divorce culture." It is the logical outcome, some claim, of a society dominated by an ethic of self-devotion brewed over the years from American individualism, social policies, and political philosophies. Divorce has emerged in the latter part of this century as a powerful institution more likely to govern family relationships than either marriage or individual obligation to family and society.[1]

Amid increasing prosperity and sweeping cultural changes, divorce became an increasingly common lifestyle choice among Americans in the decades following World War II. Census figures show that the number of divorces per year in the United States tripled between 1962 and 1982.[2] By the mid-1980s, social scientists could predict that as many as 65percent of all marriages would end in divorce.[3] Trends over the past decade show that divorce is likely to remain a lifestyle choice of about half of all young adults.[4] This pattern is difficult to ignore. It marks a radical change in American family life and represents a cultural shift in a population's values, self-understanding and community mores.

Most young Americans are likely to be affected by divorce. Demographers project that one of every two children born after 1980 will experience the end of their parents' marriage before their eighteenth birthday.[5] Research suggests that children of divorce experience a constellation of emotional, developmental, and social vulnerabilities as a result of their parents' decision. Furthermore, most divorced people remarry and form stepfamilies. And like children of divorce, stepfamily children live with their own social, emotional, and developmental vulnerabilities. If current trends continue, remarried families will outnumber intact first-marriage families by the year 2010. More than half of all Americans now living will become either stepchildren, stepparents, or stepgrandparents during the course of their lifetimes.[6]

Stepfamilies are part of a cultural revolution in contemporary America. Though they are becoming a new "norm," we have little sense of what it means to live as a stepfamily. Popular wisdom provides two attitudes. On one hand, we are lured by a shimmering, highly optimistic mirage of stepfamily possibility in motivational literature and pop psychology. On

---

[1]Barbara Whitehead, *The Divorce Culture* (New York: Alfred A. Knopf, 1996).

[2]U.S. Bureau of the Census, *Marital statistics and living arrangement: March, 1982,* Current Population Reports, Series P-20, No. 380 (Washington, D.C.: U.S. Government Printing Office, 1983).

[3]T. Castro Martin and L. Bumpass, "Trends in Marital Disruption," *Demography* 26 (1989): 37–52.

[4]Paul Glick, "How American Families are Changing," *American Demographics* (January, 1984); Paul Glick "Remarried Families, Stepfamilies, and Children: A Brief Demographic Profile," *Family Relations* 38 (1989): 24–27.

[5]David Popenoe, "The Evolution of Marriage and the Problem of Stepfamilies: A Biosocial Perspective," in *Stepfamilies: Who benefits? Who does not?* ed. Alan Booth and Judy Dunn (Hillsdale, N.J.: Lawrence Erlbaum Associates, 1994).

[6]Emily Visher and John Visher, *Therapy with Stepfamilies* (New York: Brunner/Mazel, 1996); Glick, "Remarried Families."

the other hand, accounts of stepfamily life billed as "realistic" show a shadow of impossible problems and clinical symptoms for stepfamilies. Neither of these are true to the hazy stepfamily picture developing in social science research and experience, and neither offers genuine hope to the millions of people who experience divorce and long for a second chance through remarriage.

In part, hope for divorced and remarrying families rests in a healing vision of stepfamily life that can be lived in a supportive community of faith. Nuclear families are connected to this community naturally through multiple generations of support, acceptance, and strong lines of tradition. They are familiar, and the church has attended carefully to them in its theology, teaching, and care. This is not so for stepfamilies. They are new and unfamiliar. They are theological and congregational misfits with strong negative cultural traditions and little hope of easy connection with the community of faith. It is only since the 1970s that stepfamilies have been a serious area of study for the social sciences, a task which has yet to begin for theological disciplines. At the turn of the millennium, we are just beginning to understand some of the experiences, nature, and processes of stepfamilies.

Stepfamilies in Memory and Imagination

Divorce, remarriage, and stepfamilies may be a new social norm, but prejudices about these families run deep in our cultural heritage. Most of us grew up with fairy tales and stories featuring the treachery of wicked stepmothers. The wonder of Disney animation has gifted young children with an attachment to these stories that captivates their imaginations and affects. Everyone, it seems, can feel the effects of the vicious perversion of twisted motherhood portrayed by the remarried despot who intends harm to the father's children. Generations of children have identified with Cinderella, Snow White, and Hansel and Gretel, stories that all star unhappy children abused by stepmothers. In each case, a happy ending requires the demise of the stepchild-stepmother relationship, accomplished either by stepchildren's wily manipulation or the appearance of a mythical figure (such as a prince or fairy godmother) who heals the wound imposed by stepfamily living and returns the biological father to his senses. Father, after all, has been helpless, impotent, and blinded by the evil spell of stepmotherhood.

A few counseling sessions with stepfamilies will confirm that the wicked stepmother myth is pervasive. It directs both a child's expectation and a woman's self-image as the stepmother tries to relate to a child who is biologically not her own. Deep-seated prejudices emerge when remarried women are asked to perform as they have been socialized—as household leaders, child caretakers, and limit-setters. As a pastoral family therapist, I have often heard the tears of frustrated, wounded women living in stepfamilies. Jan, a 42-year-old stepmother of her husband's three children said in one counseling session:

> I've tried so hard. We moved into a house together. We wanted to make it a home. We set up rules and schedules. We divided chores and tried to make expectations clear. The kids resented me from the beginning. If anything went wrong, it was my fault. If they had a chore, it wasn't Dad who was forcing them into slavery, it was me. When they were grounded, I was the one ruining their life. Of course, I was the one with the most daily contact with them, so I had to be the enforcer. It was so hard, but I stayed with it. I nursed them through sickness. I gave them lunch money. His oldest daughter is thirteen, and I drive her around like a chauffeur. After two years, I'm still "that woman," or "Dad's wife." I am the wicked stepmother. Any conflict with the kids, and dad comes running to rescue them from the wicked witch. I am so tired. I'm ready to quit.

Beyond stepmother prejudice, our Western heritage also provides us with deep-seated beliefs that stepfamilies will be dysfunctional. We expect self-centered stepsiblings (usually mother's emotionally overindulged children) and under-functioning fathers. "Stepchild" is synonymous with "waif" and is such an intensely biased notion that it is reserved to describe marginality, oppression, and a beggar's place in whatever good is being distributed. Moreover, negative judgments about divorced people abound, even though the odds are that most Americans will eventually be divorced. Divorced individuals are prejudged by popular and psychotherapeutic communities to be: (a) immersed in and controlled by a culture that precludes the possibility of long-term commitment; (b) self-involved narcissists unable to look beyond their own desires in order to preserve offspring and society; (c) victims rescued from the evolving abuse of bad marital choice; (d) heroic scavengers of their own personal and emotional growth from the despair of nonproductive relationships; or (e) any combinations of the above. None of these captures the complexity of every divorce, nor do any reflect the depth of divorced people's experiences.

When prejudice about divorce is added to the modern stepfamily equation, popular symbols of stepfamily life reflect deep hopelessness. Today's books and movies augment the wicked stepmother and impotent father of fairy tales with images of modern children abandoned to their own devices by self-serving mothers and fathers. In this new mythology, children raise their parents, and stepfathers molest their stepchildren. Social critics, news media, and popular talk shows portray children of divorce and remarriage as failing, acting out, and a burden to public and private resources. Daily we are convinced that you can't expect the best from children of "broken homes." Divorced and remarried families do not even get the dangerous model of the Brady Bunch and their instant love. The Bradys, after all, are a stepfamily because of death, not divorce.

These inescapable prejudices are embedded in our twentieth century literature, cinema, and popular wisdom. They impact family well-being first by determining how divorced and remarried families think of themselves, and then by influencing how stepfamilies are integrated unconsciously into communal life. Such prejudice not only disrupts a family's relational life but also has a far-reaching effect on how these families are included in the healing and redemptive life of the body of Christ. Consider a stepfamily searching for religious life in a congregation. What becomes of an inclusive invitation to the community of faith when worship leaders naively unfold biblical texts and cultural traditions that equate good families with nuclear families? Or imagine a remarried couple seeing a pastoral counselor because of marital or stepchild problems. How will they respond to unconscious assumptions and unexamined religious teachings that suggest that the divorced and remarried are incapable of the spiritual depth, love, or level of commitment typical of the first-married? Prejudicial attitudes, or silence where there is no prejudice, undermine stepfamilies' ability to find a place at Christ's table. Without an invitation actively including them, prejudice will endure and stepfamilies will be excluded.

Stepfamilies and Models of Help

Stepfamilies are complex, particularly when they are formed as the result of divorce and remarriage. What help is available? Certainly counseling and family therapy is helpful for those stepfamilies able to afford it or who are symptomatic. In the last decade a popular self-help literature has found its way to stepfamilies. Although this may signal an end to years of invisibility and a beginning for more positive images of stepfamilies, it also presents a problem. Much of this literature accentuates a simplistic, overly hopeful, and encouraging view of stepfamily life that fails to account for the radically painful experience that most encounter. Remarried families begin in loss and grief, which quickly overwhelms overly hopeful couples. Those expecting to make sense easily of their experience find themselves feeling isolated, discouraged, and unsuccessful. Self-help models generally fail to attend to long-term pervasive grief or the fact that remarriage and "blending" families will be the hardest job any family ever attempts. From statistics alone, stepfamily living is a high-risk adventure. Though census information is difficult to interpret, it is likely that less than 30 percent of all stepfamilies will survive into long-term family life. Fifteen percent of all children will live through at least two family breakups before age eighteen.[7]

Contracting for an adventure survived by less than half the participants could be seen as either insane or foolhardy. Public interest is riveted by adventures gone awry, such as guided trips to Mount Everest that result in death or defeat for a few intrepid personalities. This is the stuff of best-selling books and questions about why otherwise sensible people try such foolhardy adventures, though most climbers survive the trek and better than half eventually stand on the summit. Of course, these planned adventures are limited in scope, confront known hazards, and allow prior training and well-developed technical information and support. Only foolishness or insanity would point a weekend jogger toward the ceiling of the world equipped only with street shoes and a spring jacket. Remarrying couples, however, often embark on a trip to an uncharted wilderness with inadequate information, ill-fitting equipment, little training, and no support for the hazards along the way. Given the resources available, there is little choice except to take risks that would seem unreasonable for any other venture.

Remarrying people are not insane. Neither are they foolish. Stories gleaned from divorced and remarried people over more than two decades of counseling lead me to one conclusion. No matter how previously married people interpret their own divorces and marital histories, those trying again want what the first-marrying want. They want a family life and companionship. But more than the first-married, these couples also thirst for an added incarnation of grace that will restore faith in a relational process that has eluded them or failed them.

First-married couples often begin life together blind to their own individual dispositions, unaware of propensities toward ill-advised marital choices and family processes that are not highly conducive to relational success. They reasonably expect to grow into marital fulfillment in spite of, or because of, these complicating factors. Stress in first marriages is considered normal and a part of relational growth. Family, church, and community support systems coalesce to help these couples in their difficulties. On the other hand, remarrying couples are likely to see themselves (and be seen by their social support systems) as repeat offenders of relational misjudgment. Their motives are more likely to be maligned by their own self-assessment and by their family and friends. When normal relationship stresses appear, the remarried are more likely to interpret these negatively. Social

---

[7]Popenoe, "The Evolution of Marriage," 7.

support systems will back away and claim impotence in the face of stepfamily complexity. This confirms for the remarried that family life and companionship are out of reach for them.

Remarrying couples are not insane. They are not foolish. They do, however, enter a relational wilderness armed only with a rudimentary map marked with preliminary, vague, and uncertain landmarks. Compasses useful on other journeys are quickly found to be misleading, and there is little chance for a sustained rescue attempt should the expedition break down. Remarrying couples, at one level or another, balance personal and relational despair with a determined hope that enough grace is available to restore part of their battered dream and to sustain them through sometimes hostile territory. Pastoral care is about helping divorced and remarried families find an empowered connection with the gospel and the body of Christ that will orient them toward grace and hope in the wilderness of stepfamily living.

Stepfamilies and Congregational Care

Divorced and remarried families are fast becoming a new norm for family life. The pictures painted by statistics and individual stepfamily stories are clear. Those who live in stepfamilies need spiritual nurture and effective pastoral care. Yet resources for care of stepfamilies are absent or painfully inadequate. At the dawn of the new millennium, a review of the religious literature shows the following:

- There is no substantial writing or research of any kind in journals or pastoral care books about critically evaluated pastoral care for stepfamilies.
- Apart from a recent introductory chapter in a broader volume, no substantial journal articles or books on pastoral care and counseling treat remarried couples as a theologically legitimate, unique, or different population.
- There seems to be no attempt in the literature to explore any theology—pastoral, biblical, or otherwise—of stepfamily or remarriage.
- There is no research or speculation on religious development in stepfamilies.

At best, pastoral care of stepfamilies is guided by suggestions and a few preliminary models from behavioral sciences. Many of these are drawn from extrapolations about stepfamilies based on nuclear family processes. It is important that pastoral care providers understand that such models begin in what stepfamilies must not be and cannot be. They must not be an attempt to replicate a nuclear family, and they cannot be traditional. Other models are ambitious conceptual models describing what stepfamilies ought to be. Most of these normalize the pain of stepfamily process and try to offer some hope that problems might hurt a little less if family roles can change and stepfamily shame can be eliminated. These models, most of which are based on clinical symptoms and analysis of social problems, are an inadequate foundation for either pastoral care or a positive theological vision for stepfamily life.

Today's stepfamilies are rooted in divorce. Adults and children who live through divorce speak in a variety of languages about feeling ripped in half. In words, symptoms, and actions, they describe a systemic wound that begins in the depths of a punctured spirit and reaches outward through broken hope, relational shame, and institutional abandonment. When "family" as a central creative and redemptive metaphor to organize life is lost, a sense of futurelessness, spiritual poverty, and brokenness soon follows. This is the soil into which new stepfamilies are planted. Social and behavioral sciences can offer some conceptual distance by normalizing this pain and by reorganizing stigma attached to the experience. But there is no true redemptive vision when care is limited to calling loss gain and suggesting role adjustments. This cannot provide a redemptive vision or a path out of the tangled bondage of relational, emotional, and spiritual failure that is all too familiar to too many stepfamilies.

Divorced and remarried families begin in loss. The daily by-product of stepfamily living is recycled chronic loss. These griefs are inescapable and have deeply spiritual roots. Recovery rests in helping stepfamilies reorder life in redemptive and sustaining ways. This is a spiritual task that rightly belongs to theology and the community of faith. It is the community of faith that learns to speak of God who "acts persuasively upon the wreckage [of life] to bring from it whatever good is possible,"[8] and sees this persuasion as infinitely persistent and the greatest of all powers. Hope is more than normalization or reducing stigma. It is resurrection. It is recovery of a future. A pastoral theology well grounded in hope and resurrection must undergird any pastoral care for stepfamilies. By beginning here, the church can connect the pain and despair of stepfamily stories and their statistical futures with the embodied hope of the gospel narrative expressed in a community of faith.

---

[8]John Cobb and David Griffin, *Process Theology: An Introductory Exposition* (Philadelphia: Westminster Press, 1976), 118.

Chapter 2
Stepfamilies, Culture, and Moral Vision

In her book, *High Tide in Tucson*, Barbara Kingsolver writes:

When I was a child, I had two parents who loved me without cease. One of them attended every excuse for attention I ever contrived, and the other made it to the ones with higher production values, like piano recitals and appendicitis. So I was a lucky child too. I played with a set of paper dolls called "The Family of Dolls," four in number with the factory-assigned names of Dad, Mom, Sis, and Junior. I think you know what they looked like, at least before I loved them to death and their heads fell off.

Now I've replaced the dolls with a life. I knit my days around my daughter's survival and happiness, and am proud to say her head is still on. But we aren't the Family of Dolls. Maybe you're not either. And if not, even though you are statistically no oddity, it's probably been suggested to you in a hundred ways that yours isn't exactly a real family, but an imposter family, a harbinger of cultural ruin, a slapdash substitute—something like counterfeit money. Here at the tail end of our century, most of us are up to our ears in the noisy business of trying to support and love a thing called family. But there's a current in the air with ferocious moral force that finds its way even into political campaigns, claiming there is only one right way to do it, the Way It Has Always Been.[1]

---

[1]Barbara Kingsolver, *High Tide in Tucson* (New York: HarperPerennial, 1995), 136.

Fantasy Families

Most people who read books about pastoral care and counseling grew up in a "Family of Dolls." As both a reader and writer of such books, my own experience is a case in point. Born at the hub of the Baby Boom, I was socialized beneath an immense shadow. Looming above my budding self- and other-awareness was prosperous industrial growth, American wealth, and urbanization. Consciously and unconsciously I knew there were certain privileges and expectations that were part of the white working- and middle-class portfolio. These commonly shared expectations seeded a family norm that took root in the American Dream and are reflected in the cultural artifacts of the 1950s and early 1960s.

Television blossomed at mid-century and became a journal that articulated the expectations and vision of American family life. Through blinking electronic eyes, Americans saw that Mom and Pop on the farm no longer controlled the culture, but neither were they forgotten. Touches of cultivated lawn in clean-cut suburbs affirmed prosperity and hinted that farm-bred values had not been rejected entirely. Ward and June Cleaver, along with Ozzie and Harriet Nelson, reassured American families. Home was a warm place, nurtured by a stay-at-home mom. Carefully and lovingly she provided a retreat for hardworking Dad and two or three school-aged kids. Hot meals were served around the family table after baseball practice. Before bedtime, Dad's priority was to help Junior and Sis with homework while Mom cleaned the kitchen. Problems, disobedience, and bad influences were benign and always worked out well in the allotted thirty minutes.

In the 1970s, nostalgia about the white middle-class dream of "the fifties" captured the American public through television series modeled on a theme of Happy Days. These carefree days of self-reliant, content nuclear families were tacitly juxtaposed with the harsh realities of the 1970s. For thirty wish-fulfilling minutes a week, families could avoid the anxiety of uncertain economies, political disillusionment, post-Vietnam tensions, and gross evidence of rising family distress. Richie and Joanie Cunningham, Potsie, and Ralph reminded us what Traditional Family Values were. Divorce rates soared while metaphors with the power of gospel parables compressed our notion of "the healthy family" into a singular vision: first-married, prosperous, and striving toward insular security against a modern world filled with nuclear armaments and financial instability. By the mid-1980s, only the very privileged or very lucky could lay claim to this version of the American dream. Social and economic changes had moved a cultural icon beyond the reach of most families.

History: Demystifying an Icon

Public expectations of the family inherited from the American 1950s set a cultural standard against which all but prosperous nuclear families were judged as inadequate, broken, or nontraditional. At the end of the millennium, this vision can no longer support nuclear families, let alone nonnuclear families, which are quickly becoming dominant in our culture. Effective pastoral care with stepfamilies will require that we examine what has been called the "idolatry of the family"[2] and begin to demythologize the nuclear family. A first step is to understand that "the traditional nuclear family" is a moral construct limited to particulars of time, place, and economic circumstances of one population. It is not the Way it Has Always Been.

It is not a simple matter to explain how the American family evolved from its complex philosophical, economic, and social roots in European culture, Western religion, and early American colonization.[3] However, attending to several broad historical themes can help us construct a context for understanding the confusing moral vision of American family life since the 1950s. This brief snapshot will provide a necessary frame of reference for later chapters as we begin to listen to stepfamily stories and consider how these intersect with a redemptive moral vision for family life.

Historians[4] tell us that today's American families emerged from a heritage of nuclear households at least three hundred years old. This seems self-evident. However, a cursory historical review shows that the *nuclear household* of preindustrial society is far different from the *nuclear family* of the twentieth century. First, nuclear households were a fundamental unit of economic survival and were expected to socialize children into community expectations. Rooted in the local economy and religious structure as "a little commonwealth" or "little church," the family was a permeable structure defined more by who lived in the common house and how money and authority were managed than by strict biological or sentimental attachment. Biological children shared parents and resources with cousins, boarders, and other folk who needed a time of respite, nurture, or economic stability.

---

[2]Janet Fishburn, *Confronting the Idolatry of the Family* (Nashville: Abingdon Press, 1991).

[3]Don Browning, Bonnie Miller–McLemore, Pamela Couture, K. Brynolf Lyon, and Robert M. Franklin, *From Culture Wars to Common Ground: Religion and the American Family Debate* (Louisville: Westminster John Knox Press, 1997) identify a fourfold context of cultural change that includes first a drift in Western societies toward heightened individualism; second, the spread of market economics and government bureaucracy into family and private life; third, psychological shifts produced by these forces; and, fourth, the influences of a declining yet active patriarchy. Refer also to J. Demos, *Past, Present and Personal: The Family and the Life Course in American History* (Oxford: Oxford University Press, 1986).

[4]Tamara Herevan, "Themes in the Historical Development of the Family" in *The Family, Review of Child Development Research 7,* ed. R. D. Parks (Chicago: The University of Chicago Press, 1984), 137–77.

Unlike later nuclear families, boundaries in the nuclear household were not always obvious. Neither were they rigid or strongly defended along procreative lines. Older children and others of the household frequently moved in and out because of necessity rather than biological entitlement or developmental fiat. The systemic "glue" of the household was practical and based in social and community contract. Without the prosperity of the twentieth century, multiple laborers were required for a family to survive. Older siblings cared for the young or worked outside the home. Children supported the economy through chores. Young adults worked to support the household trade or labored at jobs within the community. Instead of a domestic retreat for a hardworking breadwinner, home was the center of economic production, the site of a common budget, and the fulcrum of mutual welfare. When able, the younger generation exited to form another household. Multiple generations rarely lived together, despite the warmth Americans in the 1970s felt about Walton's Mountain and the family cari- catured by *The Waltons* television series.

In the last century, our American understanding of human life and growth has been dominated by psychological discovery. Over this period, the idea that human life is guided by clear, sequential, and invariant organic and psychological processes has moved from theory to generally accepted doctrine. In the 1950s, sociologists expanded this notion by proposing that families also live through a stable series of predictable developmental stages. These were observed in typical middle-class American homes.[5] The family life cycle became an organizing concept for the social and behavioral sci- ences that soon guided notions about the healthy family.[6] In the 1980s, refined theories articulated a normative process of nuclear family develop- ment[7] that included two unattached adults moving through defined, ob- servable, and sequential stages: Marriage, raising young children, living with adolescents, launching offspring, living in an "empty nest," and then facing old age as a retired couple. Social scientists sometimes reminded readers that this was based on a white, middle-class population. Nevertheless, this progression has become indelibly etched in expectations for "the American family."

---

[5]Evelyn Duval, *Marriage and Family Development*, 5th ed. (Philadelphia: Lippincott, 1977).

[6]This must be qualified by the fact that historical accounts are largely restricted to white Ameri- cans. Racial and ethnic families who have maintained a rich history of extended-kin relationships are all but invisible when history is reviewed.

[7]Betty Carter and Monica McGoldrick, *The Family Life Cycle* (New York: Gardener Press, 1980). These were the first family researchers to describe and define systematically the family life cycle as a normative process. However, in 1957, sociologist Evelyn Duval published a landmark study (*Marriage and Family Development*) describing developmental tasks common to families that she believed guided individual development.

The preindustrial nuclear household was rarely so predictable or cooperative. Inconsistent contraception resulted in high birth rates. A household would often celebrate the birth of its youngest member about the same time the oldest child was leaving. Furthermore, life expectancy was short. Many children died. Men married older and died younger. Most fathers did not live to see their youngest children launched. Divorce rates were low, but economic reality prohibited divorce in most families, while morbidity guaranteed that few couples would have to sustain a thirty- or forty-year marriage.

Nurturing a healthy emotional environment for individual childhood development was not the primary organizing value for nuclear family households. Concerns about individual needs or development were secondary to the economic continuity of the household. Awareness of individual development emerged only as social changes made the nuclear middle-class family possible.

The urban middle class emerged in the nineteenth century amid changes in science, technology, economy, and a shifting psychological understanding of the self. Death rates dropped as medical treatments were developed for common diseases. Urban environments were less hospitable to large families, and lower birth rates became associated with increased productivity and prosperity. Aided by improved medical information, upwardly mobile couples opted to limit fertility. Their household roles changed as economic productivity shifted from home to the male-dominated factory, and home evolved toward a domestic retreat guarded and cultivated by women. Encouraged by budding individualism, these domestic retreats were privatized and insulated from larger social and kinship networks. The nuclear family coalesced around fewer children, who then gained emotional value as expressions of the couple's individual fulfillment and sexual satisfaction. Children were no longer a productive part of the household economy. They were instead a cherished economic liability and the primary focus of the family's sentiment, meaning, and cohesion.

Scholarship and popular attention followed this child-centered thread. Sociologists, educators, and psychologists were soon busy describing, understanding, and assisting mothers with the now critical (and female-centered) task of raising children. "Childhood," a new developmental stage, had been discovered. Scholarship was revised, and new social contracts were required. In a similar way, adolescence was "discovered" at the turn of the century as insulated nuclear families were unable to contain problematic teens steeped in individualism and disengaged from economic production.[8]

---

[8]Stanley Hall, *Adolescence: Its Psychology, and Its Relations to Physiology, Anthropology, Sociology, Sex, Crime, Religion, and Education* (New York: Appleton, 1904).

Often, certainties we take for granted take on fresh color when we attend to the ambiance of history, culture, and economic context.

Though the nuclear family ideal applied only to a minority of middle-class, white city dwellers, this idea of family grew to symbolize the hope upon which Americans built their expectations and upon which a political icon was established. This was the image of God's family proclaimed from American Protestant pulpits, even though it is rare in biblical texts. It was a vision supported by (and supporting) such important artifacts as *Father Knows Best, Donna Reed*, acid rock, and unprecedented depression among American women.

Many of us unknowingly danced before this icon as it cracked and collapsed. The musical poets of the day, eminent social critics that they were, declared their anger and discontent with the middle-class, market-driven, privileged, white lifestyle of the 1960s. Their lyrics and song titles described the death of an illusion as they tuned guitars, powered up their amplifiers, and subliminally tucked visions of decaying Victorian families into adolescent memories. Things were not as they seemed. Surrounded by middle-class wealth, Mom was tired and unappreciated. For her, life was just a bore as she waited to get old, sheltered only by the comfort of her "Mother's Little Helpers" (Rolling Stones, 1966). Dad, in his search for wealth and fame, was not around enough to warrant comment (except we are asked to have some "Sympathy for the Devil" [Rolling Stones, 1968] and his ways). Junior could find no "Satisfaction" (Rolling Stones, 1965), and, unless he was "Eight Miles High" (The Byrds, 1969), found himself in such profound despair about life and the world that he wanted nothing more than to "Paint it Black" (Rolling Stones, 1966). Sister was a "Trouble Child" (Joni Mitchell, 1974) who broke like the waves at Malibu, and in her last analysis determined that she was "Twisted" (Joni Mitchell, 1974) and would be better off dead. Oh, who's to blame? Things are just different today.

Many of us naively sang along as the guiding moral vision of our century—the Victorian middle-class urban family—creaked sideways on its eroded foundation, groaned, hesitated for one long second, and then fell with a thunderous roar and an avalanche of blinding dust.

A Culture in Transition

Massive social and cultural changes in the '60s, '70s, and '80s resulted in what Browning and his associates call "stunning transformations in American families."[9] These have produced a family environment dominated

---

[9]Browning, et. al., *Culture Wars,* 21.

by divorce, single parents, out-of-wedlock childbirth, stepfamilies, and decreased institutional support for all family forms. Browning and colleagues do not see these multiple family forms as morally neutral or simply as expressions of a plural society. Rather, they are expressions of family crisis representing failure of an organizing moral vision.

Finding a common moral vision to organize a muddle of family values, forms, and processes is no small task. Political debates of the 1990s proved that heeding the nostalgic call to reclaim the 1950s nuclear family for a new millennium was impossible, insufficient, and inappropriate. This family was homogenous, narrow, and problematic in the 1950s. It has little relevance for today's complex social context. On the other hand, progressive "normalizing" of dramatic family changes is not a plausible option. To rename divorced, remarried, and single-parent families and call them simply alternative and equally viable family forms does not make it so. This radical normalizing assumes that adults can increase their ability to choose freely between alternative lifestyles—particularly those related to divorce—without harm to either themselves or their children. This attitude became a legislative reality in the 1970s when American public policy shifted to standardize no-fault divorce. Stigma would be reduced if divorce were removed from the cusp of criminal and immoral behavior. By creating public policy that uprooted marital decision making from the loam of religious and community obligation and replanted it in more modern values of free relationship choice and contract negotiation, marital dissolution was simplified and normalized. In most states, divorce became a court-based ritual symbolizing freedom to correct marital mistakes and legally resolve couples' irreconcilable differences. Some states went so far as to produce "do-it-yourself" divorce kits. Cities featured park benches adorned with graven images of smiling attorneys hawking bargain-basement prices for uncomplicated or uncontested divorce. Legislation to expedite the divorce process was equated with helping people get on with their lives without extended, costly, and criminalizing legal battles.

Research and clinical experience in the 1980s showed that divorce is almost always traumatic regardless of popular opinion and public policy. Too often decrees were (and still are) granted unilaterally and with inadequate provision for the well-being of children or the unwillingly divorced spouse. Choice is often a one-player sport. Sometimes, too, choice is an illusion. Public policy has failed to address domestic violence adequately. Victims of violence usually have one option. They must enter the world of "alternative family lifestyles" if they want to live. It is no surprise that a growing majority of children and women live in poverty and with declining well-being.

The grim picture of "alternative family lifestyles" does not end with women and children. Studies in the late 1980s and early 1990s demonstrated that divorced folk who tried to reclaim married family life through stepfamilies risked high levels of physical, psychological, and social distress. These observations helped lead social critics in the late 1990s to conclude that patterns of adult behavior that create alternative family lifestyles are "harmful to children, costly to the nation's economy, and damaging to the well-being of the entire society."[10] With this proclamation, a new drumbeat cut across political parties and changed the cadence of the family march. Conflict around abortion and homosexuality was replaced by rhetoric to reclaim intact, two-biological-parent families as the moral norm for raising children. Millions of single-parent families and stepfamilies, close to a majority of the population, were judged by public discourse, emerging policy, and persuasive popular opinions to be inadequate, harmful, and symbolic of the self-centered cancer that is degrading American culture.

Moral Vision, Marginalization, and Care

Few children grow up wanting to establish stepfamilies. Few couples marry intending to dissolve their marriage later in favor of a more desirable stepfamily alternative. Divorce is failure, despite popular movements to soften it with words of poor marital choice, "growing apart," or irreconcilable differences. Even ending a marriage because of domestic abuse does not remove the flavor of failure. Failed marriage is rarely a badge of honor in family life. However it happens, divorce punctures a family's soul for generations and marginalizes people. We need theological and ethical ideals that can critically engage our culture and lead us to options other than divorce.

Don Browning and his colleagues in the Religion, Culture, and Family Project offer one theologically grounded moral vision. These researchers suggest that twentieth-century American culture has been dominated by a complex form of individualism that has undermined covenant, religious foundations for marriage, and support for biological parenthood. This is most evident in contractualism (which devalues marriage to the position of any other business contract) and relationalism (which evaluates the worth of marriage in what the relationship gives to individual partners). These moral frameworks cannot sustain family life. As a more hopeful standard, they propose critical familism and a critical culture of marriage. This model, the authors claim, brings church, family, and culture into a critical conversation and provides an alternative to the family disruption, nonmarriage,

---

[10]Browning et al., *Culture Wars,* 32.

and serial marriage prevalent in our time. Their analysis pans deeply into the stream of social criticism and carefully evaluates Catholic, liberal Protestant, and conservative Protestant theological traditions. From the standpoint of critical familism, the ideal family consists of

- a heterosexual couple committed to lifetime marriage,
- who parent their own children within the context of their first marriage (and so children benefit from kin altruism),
- who live out a relationship of equal regard manifested in mutual respect, affection, practical assistance, and justice, and
- who both (husband and wife) have a "public-private" life—that is, both hold privilege and responsibility in public and private spheres of life.

This moral ideal, claims Browning and his co-authors, "point[s] us beyond the immediacy of our concrete existence toward a vision for which we can hope."[11]

The work with critical familism of Browning and his colleagues is promising. It lifts up an important partial truth. It is not, however, the embodied fullness and diversity of creation. Neither is it the complete expression of the complex human experience of living in families. Moral visions are *ideal* standards around which we more or less succeed and fail. They can offer hope, but they can also marginalize. Their power to do so increases exponentially as they become the politicized "family values" standard against which people are judged.

A theologically based moral norm that points "beyond the immediacy of our concrete experience" needs a means to reconcile, restore, and heal that which is broken. At this point, critical familism fails. When a family *form* (i.e., *first-married* families) is central to the vision, there is little room for reconciliation, healing, and restoration. Those who never fit at all (never married, same-sex unions) are excluded entirely. Families of divorce are offered no avenue to reclaim a moral vision once form is broken by divorce for whatever reason. As Browning and colleagues state, the ideal is not always met. In these cases, critical familism offers the "basic social support for and connection with already existing families of single parents, stepparents, adults called to a vocation of singleness, and gays and lesbians raising children."[12] In fact, exceptions to the norm, such as families living with divorce and remarriage, require the most sensitivity from congregational care and have the most need for the inspiration that can come from an

---

[11]Browning et al., *Culture Wars,* 73.
[12]Browning et al., *Culture Wars,* 3.

inclusive moral vision. To construct a vision that welcomes "failures" and inspires hope for non-elite families will require distance from family *form* as norm.

An adequate moral vision for families must have the means for restoration imbedded in its very structure. The work of Browning and colleagues reminds us of "problematics" that complicate family life: the "male problematic" and "female problematic." These gendered predispositions rooted in human evolution chronically undermine men and women who try to embody critical familism. To take this one step further, I propose a "human problematic" that suggests that persons and families chronically *do* need, and *will continue* to need, avenues for reconciliation and restoration into renewed family life. However wonderful the vision, and no matter how hard we gaze with desire at a norm of nuclear family wholeness for all, it is unlikely we will ever embody the standard raised. When failure occurs, the same ethic that inspires equal regard and commitment must also inspire care for the wounded along with *full restoration* to a central guiding moral vision.

Critical familism, as it is now defined, cannot offer restoration. No matter how well researched, an ethic that requires single-minded judgment of the divorced and remarried and that offers no hope of full restoration loses sight of a larger picture. At the dawn of the new millennium, almost half of the American population is already held captive in Egypt. They are divorced and remarried or are living in close relationship to a stepfamily. Most are making bricks without straw. It is too late now to judge Jacob for his lack of insight and forethought in leaving the promised land for hope of better survival in Egypt. It would be easy to criticize his self-serving motives and fear of personal and family starvation. He certainly gave little thought to the possiblility that God's covenant children might be forever captive to Egypt's dominance or allure. It would have been far better for succeeding generations had Jacob stayed in his homeland, tried to work out his problems, and trusted God to provide what was needed for survival.

This is the reality of divorced and remarried people today. It does little good to vilify those who are led with or without full knowledge of the consequences into the captivity of single parenting and stepfamilies. Their struggle for survival is real enough in itself. An adequate ethic must point to God's full redemption of those in captivity. God forgives, liberates, and restores. God's love seeks to find that which was lost and restore that which was forfeited. God is not one who plays favorites to an elite class of family that has avoided divorce at all cost or who has had the good fortune of an intelligent, insightful, willing marital partnership capable of carrying out a critical culture of marriage. An adequate moral vision for families will seek to guard families against divorce and cultural erosion, but will also interpret the liberating and restoring activity of God for divorced and remarried people.

In the following chapter, I will propose a method that allows the community of faith to think theologically about God's inclusive love and how this applies to stepfamilies. This method will lead congregations to meet stepfamilies in their captivity and then explore together how God acts to sustain all families and specifically to restore divorced and remarried people to wholeness and complete participation in the body of Christ. I do not intend to produce a moral vision that competes with critical familism. Instead, I intend to articulate a way the Christian community can organize and converse in full partnership with stepfamilies to interpret the inclusive gospel of Christ in a context that includes divorced and remarried people and their struggle for wholeness.

Chapter 3
A Theological Window to Stepfamily Experience

Stepfamilies have always been with us. Yet stepfamilies at the end of the twentieth century and the beginnning of the twenty-first century are unusual. An experience that was once rooted in the death of a spouse is now mostly related to marital distress and social failure. Stepfamilies today are split families. They are complex and characterized by complicated emotional dynamics and relational structures. They are also high-risk families with dynamics that are not easy to describe and that often confuse well-meaning pastoral caregivers. Some err by underestimating the power of intricate stepfamily processes. Others become paralyzed by the intense emotional responses that are part and parcel of divorce, remarriage, and living with children that are yours, mine, ours, and theirs. Too often, this results either in no help or in advice that is simplistic and unconnected to the depth of stepfamily experience. To make matters worse, many stepfamilies are imbedded in a web of guilt and feel misunderstood, judged, and blamed. Some maintain a thin membrane of well-being, which keeps pastors, lay leaders, and others from looking closely enough to see the pain, humiliation, and stress that reside just under the surface. Other families may be honest with their pain, but then fail to respond to quick-fix strategies or interventions that miss the core of their dilemma. In this climate, it becomes easy for congregational carers to feel impotent and declare such families "help-rejecting complainers."

Pastoral carers dare not be naive about stepfamily process. Furthermore, to offer *pastoral* care to stepfamilies, intervention must reach beyond reliance on social or therapeutic sciences and dip deeply into the rich traditions of faith, theology, and congregational life. In other words, pastoral care of stepfamilies must be a multilinguistic collaboration. It must attend to information gathered from multiple sources, make living theological sense of these families' experience, and then construct interventions used creatively within congregational contexts. Creative theological imagining[1] is one pastoral method that can guide critical congregational thinking, constructive theological discourse, and strategies of care. It begins in the actual experience of stepfamilies and congregations and depends on dialogical engagement to renew theological understandings and caring action. Behavioral science research, social policy concerns, and normative moral teachings about family life provide information that is useful and important for this reflective process. However, the heart of creative theological imagining is experience itself, examined and understood in its personal, social, and religious contexts in a way that results in transforming action.

Charles Gerkin[2] proposed that the lives of those needing care resemble living and dynamic symbol systems, or "living documents." These living human documents can be interpreted through hermeneutical tools. One tool, the hermeneutical circle, is used in creative theological imagining as a transformative spiral. As we move continually around the circle, our understanding is enlarged. Deep narrative issues for the life of the soul are uncovered that move us toward increased inclusiveness in our understanding and ministry. This hermeneutical tool helps us interpret the depth of stepfamilies' experience and points us toward liberating transformation of individuals, family systems, religious institutions, social systems, and systems of care.

Stepfamilies in Captivity

Hermeneutical circularity is central to theologies of liberation. These theologies are rooted in praxis, a method that holds action and reflection in dialectical tension as the gospel is interpreted in actual social locations. Praxis generates more than understanding. The liberating gospel of Christ must be interpreted in a way that produces transforming change for particular people living in specific times and places. In reflective action, the inclusive message of Christ becomes concrete, specific, and incarnate to those who are poor, disenfranchised, or marginalized. It embodies living relief from the bondage of ideologies, theologies, and social systems that

---

[1]Loren Townsend, "Creative Theological Imagining: A Method for Pastoral Counseling," *The Journal of Pastoral Care* 50 (1996): 349–63.

[2]Charles Gerkin, *The Living Human Document: Revisioning Pastoral Counseling in a Hermeneutical Mode* (Nashville: Abingdon Press, 1984), 138 ff.

diminish dispossessed persons' humanity. It restores hurting, marginalized people to wholeness and full participation in the body of Christ. Liberating praxis does not speak *about* oppressed or marginalized people. Rather, it empowers them to interpret their situation and name hope for their particular set of circumstances.

STEPFAMILIES, SOCIAL POVERTY, AND JUDICIAL CAPTIVITY

Stepfamilies live stories filled with loss, inequity, and dispossessed hope. They are families who need restoration, transformation, and release from specific forms of poverty and captivity. Careful listening helps us hear crucial themes of stepfamily disempowerment to which praxis and creative theological imagining must respond.

Critical familism. "The New Familism" refers to a cultural "mini-shift" among maturing Baby Boomers toward reclaiming traditional nuclear family values. This movement's central purpose is to make nuclear family obligation a dominant cultural value. It places paramount emphasis on child-centered commitments and accountability, virtues that should replace the family-damaging preoccupation with self-fulfillment that pervaded the family landscape of the '60s, '70s, and early '80s.[3]

Practical theologian Don Browning and his colleagues bring some key theological concerns to familism and articulate a new normative moral vision for Christian family life.[4] I would argue that their critical familism proclaims the traditional nuclear family, tempered by shared parenting and equitable gender expectations for couples, as the Christian norm. In part, their agenda is to change social policies to support nuclear families and discourage alternative family forms. In laying their foundation for critical familism, this group critiques American family life and describes stepfamily poverty well. Their richly supported work declares that divorced and remarried families suffer specific forms of deprivation. They have irretrievably lost social capital that non-divorced families count on for child-rearing, depth of family life, and mutual care.

Divorced families, including those remarried, generally live with fewer financial resources than would be available had they never divorced. However, poverty is not limited to finances. Divorced families also suffer from lack of emotional, social, and physical support. Unfortunately, withdrawal of emotional and physical support usually strikes close to home first. Parents whose emotional reserves are decimated by divorce and its aftermath

---

[3]David Popenoe, "Fostering the New Familism: A Goal for America," *The Responsive Community* 2, no. 4 (1992): 31–39.
[4]Browning et al., *Culture Wars.*

frequently have little to give children. Parents preoccupied with personal emotional survival lose sight of their children's needs. Guilt, pain, and loss from divorce bankrupt even well-functioning adults' parenting reserves. Without these resources, difficult decisions about children become impossible. Guilt plays a trump on good parents' ability to take hard stands with children who need firm limits. Both children and parents lose. Daily survival becomes a priority over children's developmental needs.

Remarried couples often begin life together with their own form of destitution. They marry steeped in the wounds of loss. Socially, their new relationships are suspect, and they are likely to find only a fraction of the community support from friends, church, or family offered to first-married couples. Newlywed hope does not always survive its first naive blush. By definition, second (or subsequent) marriages are expected to fail.

Proponents of critical familism direct us to important truths about stepfamily living. However, scholars like Browning and Popenoe[5] want us to hear a clear negative message about stepfamilies. These and other "alternative" family forms are to be cared for, but avoided. The agenda is preventive—let's keep divorce from happening and stepfamilies from emerging. The rationale is logical—by protecting the social capital of families, quality of family life in American culture will be raised. This is a worthy goal, but it also illustrates the institutionalized marginalization suffered by those who have been divorced and remarried. It points to members of these families as socially and culturally dispossessed persons. They are second-rate leftovers.

Unfortunately, scholars invested in critical familism overlook important research that concludes that strong, stable stepfamilies are as capable of nurturing healthy development as a nuclear family and that effective stepfamilies are important in healing the wounds of divorce for children.[6] Empowered stepfamilies "work" without damaging children or undermining culture. By sidestepping affirmation of remarried families, minimizing concern for their development, and advocating exclusive social policies, critical familism participates in endangering women and children and further marginalizing an important population of families.

Women and children. Social poverty for divorced and remarried persons is weighted against women and children. This raises clear issues of justice and equality. Research into stepfamily relationships is difficult to do and hard to interpret, but several repetitive justice themes surface in the literature.

---

[5]Popenoe, "Fostering the New Familism."

[6]James Bray and John Kelly, *Stepfamilies: Love, Marriage, and Parenting in the First Decade* (New York: Broadway Books, 1998), 12.

First, it is clear that children of divorce and remarriage universally lose some depth of emotional investment from noncustodial parents. Both mother and father are less likely to invest in children with whom they do not live.[7] Frequently, parents (particularly fathers) who feel cheated by divorce settlements also withhold their financial support. Though this is a criminal act, fewer than 50 percent of children of divorce receive the child support ordered by the court. When parents remarry, marginal investment is reduced further. A phenomenon specific to fathers is "child-swapping." Studies show that remarried fathers often trade investment with offspring from one marriage for investment in the children of a subsequent marriage.[8]

Stepfamily children live with greater economic security than those in single-parent families, but studies in the 1990s show that they are also more at risk for emotional and behavioral problems than almost any other group of children. Some studies show that these problems persist into adulthood,[9] and may result from a family context that provides less warmth and poorer patterns of communication than any other family form.[10] Most frightening are studies that point to abused children in stepfamilies. One Canadian group[11] reported that children living with a stepparent were forty times more likely to be abused than other children. The same authors concluded that "stepparenthood per se remains the single most powerful risk factor for child abuse that has yet been identified."[12] The conclusion drawn by these authors is that stepchildren are not only disadvantaged; they are imperiled.

Women are also at risk in stepfamilies. Stepmothers experience higher levels of depression, fewer feelings of life satisfaction, and less internalized control of their fate than do mothers in other kinds of families.[13] Clinical observation suggests that remarried women have high expectations of marital and family satisfaction. These are short-lived. Many enjoy a brief

---

[7]Popenoe, "The Evolution of Marriage," 6.

[8]Frank Furstenberg, Jr., "Child Care After Divorce and Remarriage," in *Impact of Divorce, Single Parenting, and Stepparenting on Children,* ed. E. M. Hetherington and J. D. Arsteh (Hillsdale, N.J.: Lawrence Erlbaum Associates, 1988), 245–61.

[9]K. Kiernan, "The Impact of Family Disruption in Childhood on Transitions Made in Young Adult Life," *Population Studies* 46: 213–34.

[10]Popenoe, "The Evolution of Marriage," 6.

[11]Margo Wilson and Martin Daly, "Risk of Maltreatment of Children Living with Stepparents," in *Child Abuse and Neglect: Biosocial Dimensions,* ed. Richard Gelles and Jane Lancaster (New York: Aldine de Gruyter, 1987), 215–32.

[12]Martin Daly and Margo Wilson, *Homicide* (New York: Aldine de Gruyter, 1988) 87–88.

[13]E. Hetherington, "Family Relations Six Years After Divorce," in *Remarriage and Stepparenting: Current Research and Theory,* ed. Kay Pasley and Marilyn Ihinger-Tallman (New York: Guilford Press, 1987). See also Lawrence Ganong and Marilyn Coleman, "Adolescent Stepchild-Stepparent Relationships: Changes Over Time," in *Stepparenting: Issues in Theory, Research, and Practice,* ed. Kay Pasley and Marilyn Ihinger-Tallman (Westport Conn.: Greenwood Press, 1994), 87–125.

"honeymoon period" followed quickly by deep and extended episodes of marital and parental disillusionment.

Because of gender socialization, women often are highly invested in parenting new stepchildren. This is reinforced by biological fathers whose own gender socialization makes them more than willing to support her intentions. However, dad's "wedding gift" to Stepmom–his children–is rarely accompanied by a corresponding gift of authority or concrete support in parenting tasks. A new stepmother is left alone to parent children who resent her efforts. Without adequate support, she quickly becomes the family's "wicked stepmother" and falls heir to helplessness, depression, and assured failure.[14]

Social prejudice and political marginalization. Stepfamilies are dispossessed of family hope and heritage by American culture. The social-political statements of the late 1990s identify stepfamilies and other non-nuclear lifestyles as part of a harmful deinstitutionalization of the family, an unfavorable shift in American values harmful to children, costly to the economy, and damaging to the well-being of society. These attitudes generate marginalization. Social institutions concerned about "the family" (schools, clubs, businesses, and churches) are encouraged to organize primarily for the benefit of nuclear models. In this environment, nonnuclear families become more than just invisible. They are undesirable. They are a symbol of cultural evil and disease.

Local and national social policy reflect an attitude toward nonnuclear families that parallels sentiment about the homeless. Everyone would feel better if they just weren't there. Policies helpful to divorced and remarried families are not considered. They are too expensive, too far removed from nuclear family nostalgia, and perceived to be at odds with more important nuclear family values. Consider the following:

- There are few programs and little assistance to help children who are forced to move between homes on a regular basis.
- Parents are left alone to struggle with important transitions that deeply affect their children. Some couples and families can afford counseling. A few have access to counseling through funded agencies or providers that accept health insurance, especially if mental health symptoms appear. But unless the typical problems of divorce and remarried life are pathologized to fit into the categories of mental health services, most stepfamilies cannot readily find help.

---

[14]Edwin Friedman's parable entitled "Cinderella: An Address Delivered to the National Association of Family Therapists by Cinderella's Stepmother" is an excellent clinically informed example of women's experiences in becoming stepmothers. Edwin Friedman, *Friedman's Fables* (New York: Guilford Press, 1990), 149–54.

- It is clear that mediation helps divorced people and stepfamilies manage transitions with ex-spouses and child custody. However, there is little public funding for these services. Private mental health practitioners are usually not trained for this work, and it is rarely covered by health insurance benefits. Financially privileged families might find good services if they live in an urban center blessed with trained mediators. Where court-accessed mediation is available, it is attached to specific legal processes, staffed by overworked (and sometimes undertrained) mediators, and too often expended on couples unwilling to negotiate. By default, families are forced to simmer in problems that eventually erupt into immensely expensive legal processes.

This failure of public policy has concrete results. Children will continue to be embarrassed by school bus drivers who complain of luggage they must load so that a transition can be made between Mom's and Dad's houses. Parents will continue to have to crudely alter necessary permission forms and insurance forms to account for remarried relationships and responsibilities. Stepparents will gain no legal relationship with children with whom they have invested significant amounts of time, care, and love, sometimes for a decade or more. Children will be excluded from extracurricular activities by schools that fail to account for children who live in two houses or who must manage sophisticated agendas when one parent is absent or uncooperative. Parents who are "stuck" in divorce and remarriage transitions will continue to have no option but to argue, threaten legal action, pray for the wisdom to negotiate with an ex-spouse (knowing that if that could be done, they would still be married), or retreat to inaction. Public policy has done little to empower divorced and remarried relationships. Children are left in the middle, and responsible parents are overworked and blamed for their children's marginal performance.

Legal bondage. Perhaps the most powerful symbol of stepfamilies' dispossession is their perpetual captivity to an adversarial legal system. Relationships and identities in divorced families are forged largely in the fire of court procedures. This is true of no other family form. Custody agreements, visitation schedules, mandated child support, and religious upbringing are hammered out in court orders at great expense to all. Calling lawyers and going to court is a reality and a fearsome worry for many divorced and remarried people. Angry or controlling ex-spouses can use this threat to manipulate and intimidate. In expert hands, it promises financial ruin and absolute loss of a tenuous future with children.

Uninitiated friends, therapists, and pastors often look to the legal system as a relatively benevolent way to enforce divorce orders or resolve custody problems. Jan, a divorced mother, came in for family counseling because she was upset by her ex-husband's behavior with their children. In one session, Jan angrily summarized legal reality well:

> My pastor told me I should go back to court and demand that David have no visitation until he ends the weekend parties. In that moment, I felt so alone. He had no clue about reality for me or my family. Take it to court! I've been to court twice because David does not pay his child support. I've learned about court. My fear for my kids' emotional safety isn't going to matter. My lawyer told me that none of my concerns about David's lifestyle matter. His values don't have to match mine, and he does not have to account for his time with the kids. Without proof of child abuse or drugs, the judge wouldn't even listen to those complaints. He'd just recommend a mediator.
>
> Bottom line? I went to court about child support, and my lawyer added in a complaint about some of David's behavior. It cost me more in legal fees than the support would be if I could collect it. What's worse, the judge *lowered* David's support because I got a raise and David is self-employed and can hide most of his income. The judge did tell David that it would be a nice courtesy to tell me if he took the kids out of town again, and then gave him a lecture about paying his child support. It is a criminal offense not to pay. He could go to jail. Then he turned to me and told me that sending him to jail would benefit no one since his income would stop altogether. More than a year without a full child-support payment, and his "sentence" was to see the court mediator and outline an installment plan.
>
> I paid thousands of dollars in legal fees, and the outcome made it more difficult for me and my children. David's payments have not improved. He knows he won't go to jail. What's worse, when I press him about child support, now he threatens to take *me* back to court to get full joint custody and to stop paying support altogether. Now when I get an official-looking envelope in the mail, I get physically ill.

Pastoral carers must understand some facts about "taking it to court." First, this is rarely an option in emotionally significant disputes or for those whose financial portfolio cannot support a significant loss to legal fees. Second, courts are slow to enforce divorce- and custody-related orders, even when child welfare may be in question. By now, most family-court judges know that these disputes themselves are destructive to children's well-being. Furthermore, if one parent chooses to disregard an order, there is little judges can do to enforce it. Courts begin to appear not only costly, but impotent. Finally, though failure to pay child support is a criminal offense, support recovery is a slow, laborious process that frequently produces recriminations and ill will, but only infrequently results in criminal sanctions against those who do not pay.

When problems in divorced families result in court action, family social capital is lost to a legal system that gains its own capital by encouraging conflict. The system of law itself rests on adversarial foundations, and it encourages civil dispute. When turned toward family emotional systems, conflict deteriorates into contentious antagonism, and power is placed in the hands of combatant advocates. Everyone loses except the system itself.

At its best, our family law system is slow, ungainly, overburdened, and largely inattentive to emotional and relational nuances of family life. Judgments are made according to legislative regulation, judicial precedent, convincing arguments, prejudice of individual judges, and which ex-spouse blinks first or can no longer support the battle financially. There is no guaranteed outcome, no sure justice, and losses for children and families generally outweigh any gains won by judicial order. Even in the most consistent jurisdictions, the full range of embodied family humanity will not be considered in binding legal decisions that will affect families for years and generations. Perhaps this is best expressed in the words of a judge summarizing a custody hearing:

> The two of you are here because you cannot agree on your children's future. You have presented your best arguments and evidence. I assume you both love your children. The fact is, I don't know either of you. I don't know your children, and I don't love your children. But, it falls to me to make a decision for you according to the laws of this state. I will make that decision, and I will not make it out of love for your children or because of what I feel for either of you. The laws of this state and my best impartial judgment will determine what is best for your children. It's likely neither of you will like my judgment or get what you want from this hearing. However, you will be bound by my decision.

Judicial decision reduces love to law and imperfect impartiality. Humanity is lost. Care for children becomes a by-product of litigation, and parental love converts to mandated obligation. Child support is not a joyful expression of lavish giving to one's offspring, but punishment. Firm parenting is lacerated by fear of losing custody, and parental cooperation is transformed into a contest to retain custody. The rich complexity of life in divorced and remarried families is sacrificed to the homogenizing bondage of our legal system. Families are disempowered by its lack of sensitivity and its costs. They are held hostage by a system that cannot enforce its own decisions, that bankrupts fragile family resources, and that lends itself easily to those who would manipulate family life by threat.

EMOTIONAL AND RELATIONAL OPPRESSION

Stepfamilies are bound by a recursive interaction between social contexts and relational forces imbedded in the family system itself. Stepfamily adjustment to this multifaceted process is slow, painful, and has the potential to fragment individuals, undermine mutual family caring, and fracture fragile stepfamily alliances. The experience is most intense during the first two years of remarried life[15] and bears with it intense pain, sporadic crises, and multiple emotional and behavioral problems. Its symptoms are so universal among stepfamilies that it has become a social science standard describing "normal" stepfamily adjustment. It is also a standard that predicts a high casualty rate among remarried couples and threatens to extinguish stepfamily hope. In this context, "normal" parallels how one might describe those wounded in battle. It is normal to suffer and learn to adjust to lost limbs, diminished capacities, chronic pain, and dashed hopes. These are the probable and expected responses to unique circumstances.

This recursive interaction is also statistically normal. Since so many people live in stepfamilies and experience the chaos, pain, marginalization, and oppression of stepfamily life, it is now a statistical norm. As much as half our population will experience it. By using mathematical models and social science projections, we may now redefine the standard. Instead of destructive, life-stealing problems, the chaos and pain of early stepfamily life is usual and normal. We no longer need to be shocked or afraid when we see it. Like many forms of oppression, this adaptation of "normal" allows us to become sensitized to families' pain in ways that allow us to ignore it. It is "normal transition," not a life-threatening, hope-stealing form of bondage.

It is important for pastoral carers to understand the dynamics of stepfamily pain both as a usual response to unique circumstance and what is statistically average. It is more important that we (1) resist the temptation to accept these spirit-killing dynamics as normative *requirements* for those who have divorced and remarried, and (2) frame them within a vision of human wholeness capable of supporting divorced and remarried families outside of oppression. A vision that includes stepfamilies as part of human wholeness resists the notion that oppressive suffering is acceptable and

---

[15]Bray and Kelly, *Stepfamilies.*

unavoidable. It will try to understand and transform the processes them-selves. Without a vision for stepfamily wholeness, "normal" colludes with social poverty, marginalization, legal captivity, and religious dispossession to cripple stepfamilies before hope can take root and grow. Several distinct stepfamily processes deserve transforming attention.

Loss and grief. Stepfamily emotional and relational processes originate in divorce. They embody the efforts of wounded people to recover from trauma and claim a second chance for whole, healthy family life. However, these families begin in loss. A marriage has ended. Parents no longer live together. Animosity and blame may persist for years between ex-spouses. Life has changed forever. When divorced families remarry, this grief is car-ried into the new relationship, and divorce-related grief reverberates end-lessly through the new family's developmental cycle. This is the heart of "normal" stepfamily process. It is a spiritual, emotional, and behavioral reality that lays claim to the psyche, soul, and lifeblood of the new family and directs its paths. Adults and children are likely to relive divorce loss in repeating cycles for years, if not decades, after divorce and remarriage. One long-term study concluded that it was divorce itself, not stepfamily adjust-ment, that lies at the heart of children's problems in remarried families.[16]

Chronic stress. Any casual observer of family life knows stepfamily living is stressful. What is not so well known is that stepfamily stress is so chronic, intense, and potentially disabling that some researchers believe the costs of stress-related symptoms outweigh the benefits of remarriage.[17] All families in our culture endure a load of stress unlike previous ages. How-ever, stepfamily life is complicated by three unique dimensions.

First, stepfamily members live in a context without clearly defined family roles. Nuclear families know who "Mom" and "Dad" are. This is defined by marriage and biology. But in a remarried family, who is "Mom," or more commonly, "Jane," to children who are not related to her biologi-cally? Simply calling a parental figure by her first name in our culture sug-gests a peer relationship. Is she a peer? A parent? What is her authority? How is she to relate to the children? Who is she to Dad when conflict erupts around children? What is her role and function in the family, and who decides this? Marital roles are equally confusing. What does marriage mean when a remarried partner has to relate to an ex-spouse concerning children's support and well-being? What does it mean for a marriage when

---

[16]Bray and Kelly, *Stepfamilies*, 54–56.
[17]E. Hetherington and Kathleen Jodl, "Stepfamilies as Settings for Child Development," in *Stepfamilies: Who Benefits? Who Does Not?* ed. Alan Booth and Judy Dunn (Hillsdale, N.J.: Lawrence Erlbaum Associates, 1994).

ex-spouses, because of biological attachments, share intense feelings about children from which a new marriage is excluded? Who are remarried people as lovers whose physical attention to each other distresses offspring of another marriage? Role confusion is stressful and affects spousal, parental, sibling, and extended kin relationships.

Second, stepfamilies live in constant relational overload. The sheer number of people who must relate in some way or another grows exponentially for families who live through marriage, childbirth, divorce, remarriage, and children born to subsequent relationships. It is easy to lose track of who is "in" the family and who is not. Who is related to whom? Do stepuncles and aunts count? What about "ex" cousins or new stepsiblings' grandparents? Who should be invited to what event? Who should be left out? This can be so complex and overwhelming that stepfamily members despair and abandon relationships that could be supportive. It is hard for those who do not live in stepfamilies to comprehend how confusing relationships and roles become in the simple act of remarriage.

Perhaps the most damaging stress for stepfamilies is where grief and loss meet stepfamily confusion. This confluence produces a toxic reaction—divided loyalty—which works intrapsychically and interpersonally. Divided loyalty strangles relational growth and undermines stepfamily development. Because it is rooted in intergenerational biological attachment, it is a fact of every remarried family and is the fundmental conflict that shapes stepfamily development. It is a powerful process capable of spreading pain and toxic waste through the entire system.

Compromised couples. Remarried couples begin life steeped in remnants of past relational failure, unresolved divorce processes, and single-parent dilemmas. These add emotional weight to the newly married, which hinders their attachment process. By marrying with children, couples are also assured they will have little space, time, or permission to pursue exclusively the early sexual-marital bonding activities that will sustain them through the developmental transitions of the marital life cycle. The "honeymoon" is short if it exists at all. Newlyweds quickly fall captive to parenting, managing a household, lack of privacy, struggles with family roles, territorial conflicts, sorting out complex relationships, and simply trying to survive.

Marital bonding is compromised further by intense parent-child alliances that develop during years of single parenting. For most divorced families, survival and recovery from the trauma of divorce is successful partly because parents and children learn to rely on each other in difficult circumstances. This establishes a strong functional system that is not easily relinquished at the altar of remarriage. It is a frightening shock for many remarried couples when they have to articulate what they know viscerally: The parent-child biological connection precedes remarriage, is not shared between spouses, and has priority over their marriage. Unfortunately, this obvious fact too often lurks just under the surface of stepfamily life until it erupts violently into the open at the cue of marital conflict. Marital stress is augmented and early couple-bonding is threatened.

Parenting stress. Finally, stepfamilies lack models for effective parenting. Nuclear families have time-tested traditions that help parents make decisions about care and nurture of children. At best, these traditions do not work in stepfamilies; at worst they are destructive to children and marriages. Lacking guidance from tested tradition, parents and stepparents either fail in replicating a nuclear family or are forced to experiment. Without clear direction, adults and children pay a significant price in conflict, developmental problems, and hopelessness.

Summarizing years of research, Emily and John Visher[18] conclude that stepfamily life is more complex than any other American family arrangement. Couples remarry with hope. They bring a family together expecting restored family life. Very soon and with great vigor, emotional and relational factors contained in the experiences of divorce and remarriage work to oppress families and erode hope.

RELIGIOUS MARGINALIZATION AND DISPOSSESSION OF HOPE

Stepfamilies suffer from lost social capital, captivity to an adversarial legal system, and emotional-relational oppression. Perhaps most painful is that they are also marginalized and dispossessed of hope in religious life. Carol, a divorced seminary graduate, expresses this well:

> I wish I could find a sense of religious community for my new marriage and stepfamily. But, the truth is, the church was singularly unhelpful in my divorce. The theologies I grew up with supported that unhelpfulness and offered me nothing. As I think about marrying again, I find no reason to look forward to any church community. I don't trust it. How will my remarriage be any different than my divorce? Will I be any less suspect as a remarried person than as a divorced person? Will my church's theology be any more helpful for my remarriage and stepfamily than it was for my divorce?

---

[18]Emily Visher and John Visher, *Stepfamilies: A Guide to Working with Stepparents and Stepchildren* (New York: Brunner/Mazel, 1979), 23.

Carol's experience is common. In congregations, Christ's promise of resurrection and hope too easily converts to alienation and rejection for families faced with divorce, single parenting, and remarriage.

Most congregations do not attend to divorced and remarried family experience in liturgy, worship, or program planning. Images of the family arising in liturgy and worship will almost always assume a nuclear model, even though such families are rarely present in the biblical narrative. This is reflected in how resources are selected, how texts are interpreted, and what language is used to speak of family relationships. If other kinds of families are considered at all, they are tacked on to the fringe of worship as an afterthought, used to illustrate life's falling short of the nuclear norm, or raised as concrete examples of sin, failure, and cultural evil.

Education, music, and special-event programming can equally subjugate divorced and remarried family hope. Curricula and program planning that highlight the "best" members as those who attend church together as a family provide a profoundly negative message to children and adults for whom this is out of reach. How church leaders assign choice parts of worship, music, and drama can also represent a congregational subtext of exclusion. This is augmented by art depicting middle-class nuclear norms, traditional mother-daughter/father-son events, family enrichment programs that assume nuclear family arrangements, and celebrations that highlight the "specialness" of "alternative" families. A church unmindful of its nuclear family bias easily (and unknowingly) pushes stepfamilies away from Christ's table. When *family* is assumed to mean *nuclear* family, all others, including stepfamilies, are treated as insignificant. They have been tacitly dismissed, forgotten, and dispossessed of the hope promised by the resurrection community.

Theologies that cannot respond to remarriage or family restoration after divorce further remove hope from stepfamilies. The dilemma, of course, is how to support first-married relationships fully *and* affirm the value, worth, and dignity of divorced people and their remarriage covenants. Unfortunately, theologies of the family seem to fall into two extreme positions. At one pole, they offer a soft, uncritical theology somewhere between saying "God forgives you no matter what you have done" and claiming no moral norm for family life. This offers full and easy acceptance, but provides little normative guidance or moral expectation. The opposite pole suggests that there is no full redemption for divorced people. Remarried couples live in a conditional covenant rooted in brokenness and sin. Unlike first-married families, stepfamilies do not accurately reflect God's wholeness in creation. In this frame, first-married families are the standard for the Christian community. Divorced and remarried families are in need of religious care, but they do not share in the fullness of restored humanity and do not participate in a normative moral vision for healthy life in Christ. This theology robs stepfamilies of grace and full reconciliation with the community of Christ and with God. They are provisional families who deserve help, but no true and full welcome. They are dispossessed of hope for wholeness and divested of an inheritance.

Looking through the Window

If stepfamily care is best grounded in methods of liberation, our first responsibility is to look through frames that help us see their wounds, poverty, and captivity. They are marginalized by religious, emotional, and social powers. They are dispossessed of hope and an inheritance by theologies that exclude them. Our method of care must allow us to be touched by these realities and help us through these frames to engage stepfamilies at the deepest level of their experience. From a position of companion, pastoral care then moves with stepfamilies toward collaborative, empowering, and transforming action.

STEPFAMILIES AND LIBERATION METHODS: A THEOLOGICAL FOUNDATION

Liberation methods instruct us that social location and embodied experience are central to theological meaning-making and pastoral action. By staying grounded in concrete, particular events, religious thinking moves beyond intellectual preoccupation with individual sin and forgiveness. It turns instead to engage hurting people and acts to recover the gospel for those who suffer. These methods help the faithful community give voice to stories of the dispossessed and then together interpret their implications in the light of the Christian narrative and the work of the whole church. Through the action-reflection motion of praxis, the Christian community joins with oppressed people and families to empower transformation of their stories. New meanings, metaphors, symbols, and actions emerge that guide the community and invite suffering folk fully into the body of Christ and the hope of the gospel. Theology becomes a way of life. Faith is expressed through intelligent action that connects Christian commitment to thoughtful intervention in people's future.[19] The church's theological task is to engage stepfamilies and their stories, join with them in their struggle, empower transformation of their future, and then reinterpret the gospel in the light of a new manifestation of God's wholeness seen in transformed

---

[19]Steven Bevins, *Models of Contextual Theology* (Maryknoll, N.Y.: Orbis Books, 1997), 65.

stepfamily life. The result is not a theological "product" written by theological authorities *for* stepfamilies, but a living story of Christ's community in reflective action (or praxis) *with* stepfamilies.

Theologies of liberation are rooted in the power of praxis and transforming dialogue. Stepfamilies and remarried couples find their way out of subjugation and begin to believe in themselves only by becoming involved in a struggle for liberation and full inclusion in the body of Christ. The struggle itself is rooted in critical dialogue with and among those who are oppressed. There is no liberation without full reflective participation on the part of those who suffer. Stepfamilies and other marginalized folk cannot be directed to liberation by those who are more knowledgeable or powerful. They are not objects to be "saved." Care strategies designed with expert rescue in mind will fail or create special-interest ghettos that are easily manipulated and removed from a central place in the life of the church.

It is no wonder that pastors and religious programmers are frustrated when stepfamilies are slow to attend special programs "built just for them." As costly and well-planned as these may be, they are rarely episodes of praxis or critical dialogue. First, they are constructed by various combinations of experts—clinicians, theologians, and pastors—and rely on concepts and intuitions divorced from the daily experience of marginalized families. These well-meaning professionals write programs that are then injected with authority into the world of stepfamilies who attend church. Remarried couples are rightfully slow to trust the "liberating" advice of religious authorities who helped marginalize them in the first place. Do these same people now hold the answer for their new remarried status? Second, oppressed remarried couples live with chronic fatigue. Special programs usually require already overloaded families to make extra (and sometimes exceptional) effort to attend activities separated from their normal routines. These are likely to be dismissed as requiring more than they give. Finally, by giving stepfamilies "special space," church leaders short-circuit critical dialogue and remove stepfamily stories from the broader gospel narrative. Conversation takes place not between stepfamilies and the rest of the church, but in specialized enclaves of homogenous folk talking together alone. Divorced and remarried people are removed from the central fabric of religious life. Their contribution to the core meaning-making activities of liturgy, worship, education, and community conversation are lost to a special-interest ghetto. In the end, the church avoids transformation and misses an opportunity to fulfill its mission to stepfamilies.

The church is to be about liberation of those who are marginalized and oppressed. Too often, church leaders have looked to specialists and authorities to provide answers about health, healing, and recovery for problem populations. However, liberation and transformation are rooted not in the best constructions of experts, but in praxis that leads the oppressed toward their own empowerment.[20] Praxis is not a mystery. Neither is it a special tool reserved for liberation "specialists." Instead, it is a human fundamental. It is in action whenever people are creating meaning—in stepfamilies, churches, homes, and work. Humans consider the world, understand it, and then transform it. Human activity *is* praxis. It is action *and* reflection, theory *and* practice rooted within a community making sense of its own experience. When this action-reflection dialogue takes place in the presence of profound love, like that modeled by Christ, it transforms the world.

When the church reflects on Christian praxis in the light of the word of God,[21] a special kind of dialogue takes place. It begins with belief that God acts in history, is revealed in everyday events, and is not neutral. It proceeds as people of faith circulate through an action-reflection cycle to locate God in the embodied life of oppressed people and then cooperate with God in healing, reconciling, and liberating. In this cycle, the people of God are drawn to God's transforming purposes, to change the social institutions, religious structures, values, practices, and policies that keep women, children, and men from human wholeness and from full participation in the body of Christ.

Praxis is more than a way to cause change. It is a way of forming, or *trans*forming, a mutual future that allows a deeper and more challenging knowledge of God for both the oppressed and the oppressor. It is a concrete way of being Christian that is authentically spiritual. It calls us into critical dialogue and solidarity with the oppressed as a form of prayer, and identifies us as peacemakers in search of shalom.

Ministers, pastoral carers, and counselors are not authorities who act on or for stepfamilies needing restoration. Instead, they are to be midwives of theology by ordering praxis, providing it with the perspective of the Christian tradition, helping people apply it to their lives, and then articulating new theological meanings more clearly.[22]

Robert McAfee Brown outlines a general format for ordering praxis in congregations:[23]

---

[20]Paulo Freire, *Pedagogy of the Oppressed* (New York: Continuum Press, 1993), 107.

[21]Gustavo Gutiérrez, *A Theology of Liberation* (Maryknoll, N.Y.: Orbis Books, 1980), xxix.

[22]Bevins, *Models of Contextual Theology,* 68.

[23]Robert McAfee Brown, *Gustavo Gutiérrez: An Introduction to Liberation Theology* (Maryknoll, N.Y.: Orbis Books, 1990).

- First, praxis avoids abstraction. It must be related to specific praxis situations affecting real people in daily life. It is grounded in *everyday experience* of the world in concrete social locations.
- Second, the action-reflection/thought-action motion of praxis is *always* for the purpose of transformation. Truth is something that is done, not discovered or uncovered.
- Third, praxis is not about finding solutions and imposing these on oppressed people. Rather, it is about empowering the oppressed to change their own situations.
- Fourth, praxis is not a solitary project. Instead, it is the activity of a community engaged in an intentional cycle of action and reflection.
- Finally, praxis and critical dialogue are never complete. As a method of constructive theology, it contains the tools for ongoing correction and avoids settling into a rigid orthodoxy.

STEPFAMILIES, PRAXIS, AND HERMENEUTICAL CIRCULARITY

Creative theological imagining with stepfamilies is grounded in the Christian community and carried out through praxis and critical dialogue. The action-reflection motion of praxis interprets the gospel within the concrete social reality of stepfamilies and drives the circle of liberation and transformation. This teaches us what pastoral care means. "Hermeneutical circulation"[24] draws us into experience with marginalized people, forcing us to challenge our ideological captivity. The "motion" of reflection and action, understanding and change must lead us to suspect ideologies that shield us from hard realities and allow us to be complacent about others' suffering. When our vision is clouded by nuclear-family ideology, we are shielded from the painful reality of divorced and remarried people: Stepfamilies exist; they are not going to disappear; and they endure high levels of suffering, marginality, and disenfranchisement.

Nuclear-family idolatry would have us minimize this pain or relegate it to suffering deserved because of poor choices. However, when stepfamily realities are brought together with the message of the gospel, we face a choice. We either discount the divorced and remarried as unworthy of wholeness and inclusion, or we are drawn into a life of faith that "sees no neutrality is possible, and recognizes that revolutionary praxis can lead to theological creativity, in which a new reading of the Bible and Christian tradition can emerge."[25] If we choose the latter, hermeneutical circulation

---

[24]Robert McAfee Brown, *Theology in a New Key: Responding to Liberation Themes* (Philadelphia: Westminster Press, 1978).

[25]Ibid., 59.

requires that we become theological actors and reflectors with stepfamilies and alongside God. This is redeeming care. It saves stepfamilies from superficial "help" and rescues carers from unreflective "helping" that is disengaged from those in need, selfishly soothes our anxiety about people in pain, and then lets us in good conscience avoid any true transformation.

Hermeneutical circulation, praxis, and creative theological imagining is the harder way. It draws us close to the experience of hurting, disenfranchised people and insists we stay close, even though their pain may make us anxious. This is threatening, but to engage and reflect, we must name stepfamilies' pain and our mutual complicity in that pain. We will be forced to ask hard questions about God's radical demand for justice and inclusion and then explore how these principles apply to non-normative, marginalized families. Stepfamilies and those who care for them will change. Congregations and the theological symbols and meanings they embody will also change. This harder way, of course, is subversive. It requires that we turn expectations, rules, roles, and hierarchies upside down in anticipation of a new language of hope and new visions of justice. It means we will have to face a constant tension between tradition, biblical text, and a new understanding of experience caused by the creative, reflective activity of the community of Christ.

Creative theological imagining is about opening our eyes and seeing stepfamilies, perhaps for the first time. It is about a connection with these families that follows Jesus' thoroughly engaged praxis of eating with outcasts, touching lepers, and destabilizing exclusive hierarchies that chain the means of grace to ideology and right form. Engagement at this depth begins by seeing the full complexity, mystery, and difference in the other. This happens best through what Sallie McFague has called "the loving eye," which comprehends that the other has its own integrity and interests. The loving eye must look and listen, check and question. It does not assume that *my* best interest is the other's best interest. It does not expect that *my* experience is the other's experience. The loving eye respects the experience of the other and expects that knowledge of the other is "…slow, open, full of surprises, interactive and reciprocal, as well as attentive to detail and difference."[26] It is also tough and able to acknowledge the difficult truth that reality includes others.

Perhaps most important, the loving eye can "lock eyes" with another and enter into a subject-subject experience that deeply recognizes the intrinsic value, worth, and connection between two subjects. This is the lovers' mutual

---

[26]Sallie McFague, *Super, Natural Christians: How We Should Love Nature* (Minneapolis, Minn.: Fortress Press, 1997), 34–36.

gaze and a mother's intense connection with her nursing child. It is a relationship that "knows" through engagement with another.

"Knowing through relationship" is a method used by feminists, ecologists, phenomenologists, and process philosophers. It is a way of knowing that preserves the integrity of the other by claiming that who and what we try to understand is truly a subject worthy of respect. It is harder to dismiss, to use, or to study individuals and families objectively when we acknowledge their experience as valid, valuable, and important. This kind of engagement calls us to friendship with stepfamilies and asks us to be in relationship with them. It asks us to learn about who we are together, first-married, not-married, and remarried. What are our respective places in the world of family life, religious life, and cultural life? What meanings grow out of being remarried, and how can first-married and remarried families' lives be mutually enriched in this relationship? How is the body of Christ revealed in each? How does God's saving power become a daily reality for remarried couples and stepfamilies? What does this say about God's activity and presence in the world? How is this different from first-married families, who more closely fit the accepted religious and moral norms?

If we are unable to see the differences between ourselves and another, or between one family and another, it is because we have not bothered to look or listen closely. Hermeneutical circularity, praxis, and the critical dialogue of creative theological imagining ask us to look closely at others' subjective experience, listen carefully to their story, and know them through relationship. This involves more work than simply listening to them, for them, or about them through statistical inferences or popular notions. Friendship with stepfamilies is engagement at a concrete, local, and messy level. It is seeing that transcends mere observation, hearing that exceeds objective listening. These happen, for instance, when a child's angry eruption meets our heartfelt empathy. Instead of impersonally judging parent and child or making a quick suggestion about better discipline, we make an effort to understand both stepchild and stepparent's unique experience and begin the process of relational knowing. Friendship with stepfamilies crosses a threshold and attends with respect and care to the stories of particular problems, joys, and heartaches that can be found only in remarried relationships.

Knowledge anchored in everyday relationships with stepfamilies jars us quickly beyond theologies of family life and care strategies that depend upon traditional nuclear family experience. Helpful "chicken soup" cliches that are time tested with non-divorced families have little to say to divorced and remarried families. Instead, empathy and relationship will press us toward "practical knowledge with the goal of responding to the other in terms of their own well-being."[27] This kind of relationship asks us to engage stepfamilies in their daily life and experience their intensity and differentness. We will be unsettled. Our confidence will be shaken as we find our guiding theologies and moral norms inadequate. This is a risky, adventuresome thing. It forces us beyond reified and petrified theological metaphors that have historical meaning but which are now unable to interpret the saving, restoring love of God in powerful and pervasive ways to families who are different.[28] Praxis demands that we press the boundaries of religious tradition in order to interpret God's radically inclusive love to divorced and remarried families.

The flame of creative theological imagining is ignited within a community of faith (or an individual pastoral carer) when traditional sensibilities are confronted by a "jarring" experience that exceeds the boundaries of their understanding (see fig. 1, step one). This may happen when a stepfamily's pain makes its way into a family crisis, a church meeting, or the pastor's office. Under adequate pressure, most families' defenses will falter and eventually fail. When defenses fail, people act in ways that are unfamiliar or frightening. Stepfamilies are predisposed to faltering defenses and are exceptional sources for unforeseen challenges to traditional sensibilities, community jarring, and potential "loving eye" experiences. Unfortunately, these jarring opportunities to begin hermeneutical circulation and creative theological imagining are usually lost. It is easier for pastors and congregational leaders to forget about friendship, deflect the problem with a counseling referral, and become overreactive or paralyzed by taking expressions of pain personally.

To move beyond the first step of an awakening jar and into a different way of knowing is not easy. It requires that we hear, see, taste, and feel a remarried couple's attempt to define and defend their existence, identity, and worth. Engaging awareness is the second step of hermeneutical circulation (fig. 1). At this point, we move beyond simple recognition that our traditional sensibilities have been breached and into the territory of new discovery—listening to stepfamily stories and beginning to know them relationally. If step two is successful, the community of Christ will tumble headlong into the crucible of Jesus' subversive, destabilizing praxis to awaken alongside stepfamilies in their pain and confusion. Together, we will ask questions about exclusion, inclusion, justice, and hope. These collaborative

---

[27]McFague, *Super, Natural Chrsitians,* 38.

[28]Sallie McFague, *Models of God: Theology for an Ecological, Nuclear Age* (Minneapolis, Minn.: Fortress Press, 1987), 44.

conversations at Christ's table, while intense, hold the hope of new meanings, symbols, and rituals. They will reach beyond reified and petrified theological metaphors and toward a reinterpretation of God's inclusive love for stepfamilies and the congregations in which they live.

Hermeneutical Circulation

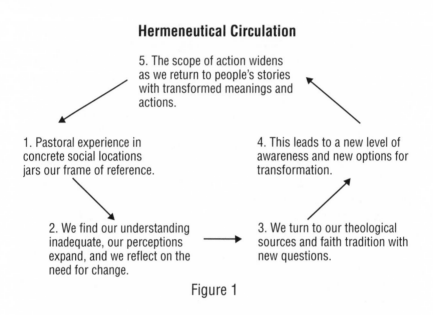

Figure 1

Step two of hermeneutical circularity listens carefully to particular stepfamily stories and to the research, clinical literature, and popular culture, which gives us a broader view of stepfamily life. By listening, we soon find that there is no particular "map" for what stepfamilies experience. We also discover that there is no unified cluster of behaviors, characteristics, or processes that we could safely call a symbolic model of "the stepfamily experience." Instead, we find only vague themes of adjustment, grief, psychological homelessness, and change, which seem common to divorced and remarried couples and their children. But the moment we assume that all, or even most, stepfamilies' experiences are identical or highly similar, we miss the complexity, depth, richness, detail, and intensity of a family in its particularity. The second step of hermeneutic circulation helps us avoid the trap of overgeneralization by asking us to engage stepfamilies in their particularity. With an attitude of discovery, we are charged to watch and listen, to learn from what is around us and from our engagement with the daily details of stepfamilies.

To open ourselves to stepfamilies (step two) requires that we transcend our self-absorption and our prejudices, biases, and projections about remarried persons and life in stepfamilies. This is an act of spiritual discipline grounded in an active community of common worship. Transcending one's own ideological bondage in order to see another more clearly is not a solitary task assigned to a professional minister or carer. Instead, it happens when members of the body of Christ collaborate in meaningful ritual, spirit-quickening stories, and life-giving reflective meditation. These shared commitments and disciplines help us avoid captivity to predictable, linear, and objectively rational knowledge about stepfamilies. When the community anchors its dialogue with stepfamilies in an active life of prayer, meditation, and faithful sharing, knowledge transcends objectivity. It becomes deeply subjective and personal.

Conversations with stepfamilies that begin in meditative reflection move us beyond knowing *about* stepfamilies and into *knowing* stepfamilies. The self-transcendence of common worship stimulates a right-brained, analogical process that allows us to have "mini-*kairos*" glimpses of the complex realities of stepfamilies. These are beyond rational, logical thought. Shared meditative reflection draws us to an intuitive connection with the spiritual-emotional "whole" of stepfamilies and disengages us from the hegemony of linear, intellectual, fragmented images that come to us through logical observation. This, in turn, taps a deep well of religious imagery that expresses the life struggle common to the whole community of faith and for which the gospel must be newly interpreted in various times and places. The community struggles for shared meaning in the light of God's inclusive love for stepfamilies and moves toward the resources of faith for regenerated understanding.

Step two of hermeneutical circulation forces us to be more than spectators. If we are to be integrated carers, we are pilgrims with and collaborative listeners to stepfamilies. We will care enough to hear particular voices, unique songs, and specific laments. Through mutual spiritual connections, we will learn to understand the meanings of stepfamily songs in the context in which they arise. We will take the time to observe the complexity of changing keys, lyrical shifts, and the difference between dance and dirge. We will be captivated by stepfamilies and their hopes, their dreams, and their pain.

Once we are jarred and make the commitment to a reflective relationship with stepfamilies, we are driven to our theological sources and faith traditions with new questions (fig. 1, step three). What are we to make of the specific themes we find in the melodies, harmonies, and dissonances of stepfamily life?

It is not enough to apprehend the complexity of stepfamily life in a Christian context. The community is also called to respond. But this is too simple. The community is called to a caring, redemptive response that is rooted in the praxis of Jesus' life, ministry, and resurrection. It must respond in a threefold way. It must first engage stepfamilies in the immediacy of their crises, suffering, and joy. Action becomes part of engagement, as the faithful community relies on its theological memory and gospel heritage to guide a relational response to immediate pain. Finally, contained in this engagement is a spoken and lived hope that expects God not only to contain crises but also to transform the future for both stepfamilies and the church. Steps three and four of hermeneutical circulation engage stepfamilies at the messy level of crisis and look beyond this to a liberated future. These two steps are locked together in a recursive, mutually interpretive dialectic that is active, theological, and creative. It is here that theology is "written" with stepfamilies. Contained within the faithful community, stepfamily stories and the central Christian narrative are brought together with renewed attention to what these stories together tell us about transformation, human wholeness, and God's inclusive, liberating love.

Care in the community of Christ molds new meaning for itself and for its stepfamilies. By paying particular attention to religious tradition and new information from divorced and remarried people in daily life, theology becomes a reflective activity. It avoids unconscious dogmatism—McFague's "reified and petrified" theological metaphors—and brings new life to issues confronting the Christian community. Together, stepfamilies and congregations face troubling questions raised by lived experience. Together they engage in critical dialogue, explore how central gospel meanings intersect with troublesome questions, and then imagine transformed futures grounded in the liberating gospel of Christ. As the church lives into redeemed visions for stepfamilies, praxis keeps the community rooted in active reflection, in which new futures are tested, redemptive meanings and metaphors are honed, and inclusive symbols are ritualized. The theology and practice of the church is broadened as new meanings, metaphors, symbols, and rituals are incorporated into its life and transform its pastoral action (fig. 1, step five).

Creative theological imagining is a continuous, recursive process of the church. It is constructive theology, which, after all, is an activity of the whole church. It is not restricted to a special group of professionals skilled in writing. As John Cobb reminds us, theology is simply "intentional Christian thinking about important matters,"[29] such as stepfamilies. For our purposes, creative theological imagining will provide a frame to:

- listen reflectively to stepfamily stories,
- understand and empower a voice for divorced and remarried families' stories,

---

[29]John Cobb, *Lay Theology* (St. Louis: Chalice Press, 1994), 12.

- point to traditions of redeeming hope in the body of Christ to enliven transformation of stepfamilies and congregations,
- discover metaphors, symbols, and rituals of hope for stepfamilies through the process of action-reflection,
- articulate a vision for stepfamilies' full inclusion in the life of the church and into a redemptive moral vision of family life, and
- explore a beginning theology of remarriage and stepfamilies capable of including divorced and remarried families as part of the embodied fulness of creation and incarnation.

Part 2 of this book will focus on stepfamily stories. These provide the raw material for "jarring" a congregation's consciousness and will press us to examine some central Christian metaphors that intersect with stepfamily themes. Chapter 8 will provide a speculative case study that illustrates how stepfamilies and a congregation can move through hermeneutic circularity, implement praxis, and use creative theological imagining to renew symbols, ritual, and pastoral care.

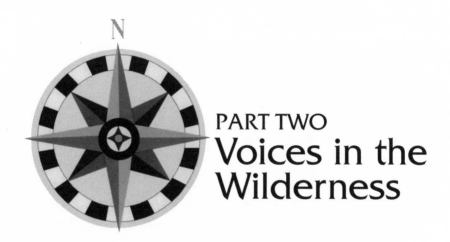

PART TWO
Voices in the
Wilderness

Chapter 4
Remarried Families, Loss, and Grief

What's in a Name?

Few words evoke more prejudice or emotional reaction than *stepfamily*. It is not a happy term. It is a word to be avoided, even by popular word processing spell-check programs. The one I use strongly resists reprogramming to accept the title. On a more human front, I have lost count of the number of workshop speakers and lecturers who circumvent the word *stepfamily*. Without much reflection, many have simply grasped a more fashionable name for these "alternative families." Others have professed great thought about rescue strategies for remarried families and have used intricate conceptual contortions and condescending reassurances to spare clients, parishioners, students, and friends the damage of being called a stepfamily. In recent years, social scientists and self-help authors have tested new names and divergent views of divorced and remarried families. *Blended family, binuclear family*, and *reconstituted family* have each had a turn as the popular new symbol for remarried life. These and other terms were expected to redefine what it means to try again after divorce. With a new reality, couples and children might feel the loss of nuclear family less and gain hope about being an alternative (not inferior) family. Names, after all, both reflect and create reality. Isn't it better to create a new, less prejudiced reality than to struggle with an outmoded title carrying historical baggage?

New and popular names come with their own troubles. What is to be blended in a "blended family"? How is it done? What should the outcome look like? No one is quite sure. Clinical experience suggests that individuals living in remarried families, while drawn to the concept of *blending*, are resistant to it. Too, *blending* anticipates more loss of pre-divorce relationships and attachments. Both children and adults resist the aggravation of old wounds brought on by encouragement to blend. Remarried families that approximate blending are not common and represent individual style rather than appropriate goals for stepfamily success. To expect that successfully remarried families eventually will blend smoothly together is counterproductive. It is more realistic and constructive for remarried families to retain their diversity, encourage individual character among family members, and learn to manage troublesome leftovers from previous attachments.

Binuclear has also been used to describe stepfamilies. This notion keeps remarried families a step closer to the nuclear ideal and avoids the messiness of nuclear family dismemberment. Remarriage could reconstruct a new family organization along nuclear family lines with not one, but two nuclei. Conceptual reorganization around dual nuclei minimizes divorce losses and holds family processes together through multiple relationships and across marriages. Furthermore, common nuclear family constructs could be retained to understand and study remarried families.

Binuclear may describe some remarried constellations. However, the concept has had little appeal to either stepfamilies or scholars. The term may avoid prejudice, but it is a cold, sterile, clinical neologism that sparks little passion. Conceptually, it fails to approximate the experience of most couples and children living through divorce and remarriage. It also fails to provide any realistic, attainable normative vision for remarried families. Experiments calling divorced and remarried families "reconstituted" are equally uninspiring. It is a confusing term with no clear meaning or definition. The word literally means to set up again, which brings to mind reconstruction or reenactment of the original family structure. Reconstituted orange juice closely approximates the original product. Remarried families, on the other hand, resemble nuclear families in some ways, but clearly are not the same. As a descriptive name, *reconstituted family* offers little to help us understand stepfamily process or assist remarried couples and children in managing new relationships.

A common thread binds these experiments together. They all seek to avoid prejudice while describing a particular family experience. But more importantly, they also minimize the reality of enduring loss, pain, and grief, which gather at the heart of families who are divorced and remarried. These folk are, first and foremost, *stoep* families. *Stoep* is a word that has survived from old English and means loss. Stepfamilies are rightfully families of loss.

The term *stepfamily* is worthy of redemption. It speaks as no other term can to the cycle of loss, grieving, recovery, and recapitulation that drives stepfamily life and development. This is a defining reality for those who have lived through divorce and family reorganization. To underestimate its power in stepfamily life is to overlook an obdurate and constant companion with which all remarried couples and their children live. This palpable entity sleeps in remarried couple's beds, hides in their children's closets, and springs from behind the veil of unconscious family process at the most sensitive, vulnerable, and important life events. It must be taken seriously as an organic, ongoing force in stepfamily life. To offer effective pastoral care for stepfamilies, loss and grief must be named. Its embodiment must be recognized, and its fullness encountered within the healing and restoring body of Christ.

A Geography of Loss

Divorce-related grief is not metered to conclusion in a matter of months, years, or decades. Neither does successful grieving come with a return ticket to familiar pre-divorce territory. Divorced persons cannot return to the conventional, civilized world of the first-married or unmarried. Remarriage is profoundly affected by this fact. Successful stepfamily living does not mean surviving a year or two of predictable adjustments that then lead back to well-traveled nuclear family paths. Instead, remarriage is tightly bound to permanent changes in family and individual life cycles. Divorce loss and remarriage hope are interwoven into a lifelong tapestry where beginnings and endings meet by accident and where a cry of joy unerringly and without warning touches a moment of deepest sorrow. Stepfamilies are born in a wilderness where past and future collide and ghosts inhabit the land. *Stoep*, or loss, resides constantly near the stepfamily's heart. A vignette from a pastoral counseling case illustrates how grief and loss chronically affect a stepfamily's life cycle.

Ilene came in for her first counseling session just weeks after her thirty-fourth birthday. In her first session she described feelings of helplessness and hopelessness that we together defined as depression. Though not surprised by this diagnosis—she had suffered from depression many times before—she was unsettled by it. Life was coming together for her in very promising ways. Why was she unhappy when there was so much hope in front of her?

As Ilene's story unfolded, a familiar picture emerged. At age 31 her marriage of six years ended when her husband became sexually involved with a colleague at work. The couple entered marital therapy. When she discovered that Dan had lied about ending his affair, Ilene filed for divorce. Since the divorce was uncontested, the legal process itself was not difficult. However, recovering emotionally from Dan's betrayal and loss of her marital dream was much harder. She remained in personal therapy to manage the effects of divorce. By the end of her first year post-divorce, Ilene felt enough control of her emotional life to terminate sessions with her therapist.

Looking back, Ilene felt good about her three years as a single parent. She had provided a home where four-year-old Amy had thrived, and she was financially successful in her marketing career. Amy was doing well in school. Her own network of friends was intact, and she was now considering marriage with a wonderfully attentive man whom she had dated for eight months. So, wondered Ilene through angry tears, what was the problem? Why was she depressed?

In subsequent sessions, Ilene explored her depression in the context of her family history. Her genogram showed that she had been born in a suburb of a large city in the western United States. She was a middle child with one brother two years older and one thirteen months younger than she. She talked about her siblings warmly and recalled many times when they acted as her "bodyguards." Though they lived some distance from her, she had frequent contact with them and enjoyed their visits. During her divorce, her brothers "stood by me in my time of need."

Ilene believed the defining event for her family of origin was her parents' divorce when she was six. Her parents were "children of the early 1960s" in suburban America. They grew up in privileged homes, played all the right sports, attended dances, and graduated in the top half of their high school classes. Both attended a large state university, where they met in the late 1960s. A whirlwind courtship during "the summer of love" resulted in pregnancy, marriage, and a subsequent miscarriage. As a young child, Ilene remembers her parents' distance from each other and occasional fights. Her mother, she felt, was chronically unhappy and took prescription medication for her "nerves" through most of Ilene's childhood. Her father worked long hours as an engineer, while her mother worked part-time in a floral shop and cared for the children. Ilene knew that her mother wanted to be a psychologist but had never pursued graduate education.

In 1974 Ilene's parents divorced. She remembered coming home from school one day to find her mother tearfully packing bags. Ilene and her brothers were told only that they were "going to live with grandma for a while." One month later, her mother told the children that they would not be returning home. She and dad were divorcing. They would now change schools and move into grandma's house permanently. Ilene spoke of a two-year legal battle that kept the entire household, including grandma and grandpa, in a continuous outraged uproar. She remembered long episodes when she and her mother shared tears. Her jumbled childhood memories were filled with adults' angry outbursts about her father, anxiety about the sale of the family home, and her own sadness about her father's absence. She remembered thinking that dad had horribly broken some rule. He was banished from her life, and she was supposed to be better off without him. Ilene's suspicions about her father's affair were confirmed when she was 14. As a child she lived in confused vacillation between guilt at missing her father badly, angry collusion with her mother against her father, sadness, and shame about her parents' divorce.

As we traced Ilene's history, we quickly found phantoms of divorce at every developmental stage. Her performance was so bad in second grade that her teacher recommended she be held back. An old report card suggested that she had trouble concentrating, could not sit still, and brooded alone during play times. Her teacher thought she lacked the maturity to enter third grade, but Ilene's mother insisted she was only adjusting to her new life. She was not held back, but her grades remained marginal. Ilene concluded she had been depressed and fearful through most of her early childhood. She remembered feeling disconnected from life and at times, "like my guts had been cut out."

Ilene entered junior high school at age 12. Two months later her mother announced her upcoming marriage and was angry when her children reacted with less than joyful enthusiasm. Looking back, Ilene could articulate her anger and sadness about her mother's marriage. First, it symbolized the final rejection of her father, who had not remarried and now had regular visitation with his children. Second, her mother's marriage meant that she would lose the familiar home she had with her grandparents. Soon after her mother's marriage, Ilene began failing in school. She was "rebellious and defiant," began smoking, and "gave mom hell." Intuitively, she knew she was the cause of her mother and new stepfather's frequent arguments.

Midway through seventh grade, Ilene was referred for psychological treatment. She was diagnosed as "oppositional" and treated with a contract-driven behavior modification program. This was designed by her counselor and delivered by her mother and new stepfather. She remembers rarely talking to her mother, withdrawing from family life, hating her stepfather, defying her counselor's efforts, and wishing she could live with her dad. She had not gained a stepfather, but lost a mother. Mom was not as available as she had been, and now she frequently deferred decisions about

Ilene to "that guy," her new husband. Ilene resented his intrusion into her life. Throughout seventh grade, she had a recurring dream in which her parents remarried. Counseling was discontinued for lack of concrete results.

Ilene's graduation from junior high school was a "disaster." Her accomplishment was overshadowed by open hostility between her father, mother, and stepfather. After the ceremony she sat behind the school gym with her older brother and cried. Her mother had withheld invitations to her graduation from her father and his girlfriend. As a result, Dad had not been admitted to the auditorium. Outraged, he had forced his way past security guards to stand in the back of the room, too late to see her receive her certificate. At that moment she vowed to trust no one to be honest with her. She concluded that people protected their "rights," even to her life, before they cared about what she felt or needed. She commented, "at the same time people were fighting over me, I never felt so alone in my life."

High school was a "blur" for Ilene. With more freedom, she spent less time at home. Because of troubles between her mother and stepfather, she could easily manipulate her mother into inadequate supervision. When her mom was preoccupied with problems in her marriage, she paid less attention to Ilene. When her stepfather tried to intervene, Ilene became defiant and angry, and intentionally sparked conflict between her mother and stepfather. Her mother's resulting sense of hopelessness and helplessness freed Ilene further. When extra fuel was needed to free her of parental encumbrance, she did not hesitate to triangle her father into the conflict. Comments beginning with "well, *Dad* lets me..." were usually sufficient to ignite the necessary flame. Her dominant memory of high school was anger, punctuated by lengthy dark periods of sadness. These were remediated only by occasional drinking binges and intense romantic encounters that became increasingly sexual. She soon discovered that her developing body and sexual responsiveness could attract and keep male attention in a singular and unparalleled manner.

Episodes of romance alleviated Ilene's anger and helped her feel attached to another person. Unfortunately, most of her relationships were short-lived. When they failed, she felt cheated, hurt, and more alone. This process was embodied when she became pregnant in her senior year of high school. Her boyfriend accepted no responsibility for the child. He denied having sex with her and suggested that any one of six or seven other young men might be the father. Terrified and humiliated, Ilene aborted the pregnancy. She never told her mother or her father. Her father, after all, was in the throes of early remarriage, and her mother was working as hard as possible to preserve a marriage Ilene felt responsible for endangering. Her older brother knew of her pain and promised to take her secret to his grave. He also beat her ex-boyfriend senseless in a convenience store parking lot.

High school graduation was a repeat of her junior high experience. She made sure both sets of parents had pictures, tickets, and seats. However, post-graduation activities were again filled with overt hostility between ex-spouses and competition for her time and attention. She remembered feeling "Hey! Who's this about anyway?" She did not speak these words.

After high school, Ilene attended a local college. Facing the challenges of adult expectations—Mom had been clear about her need to leave home—Ilene experienced her first episode of severe depression and anxiety. According to her own account, she had barely finished high school. Now she was faced with no "safety net" of parents who were responsible for her or to whom she was even marginally accountable. They both had their own lives, and hers felt empty. Her attempt to fill it with a man again ended with her heart broken once she had committed her body to the relationship. She found herself sick of life, relationships, school, and herself. In what she later saw as a suicidal gesture, she retreated to her bedroom and remained for a week without light, food, or outside contact. Frightened by her behavior, her roommate physically forced her into a car and drove her to the college counseling center.

For two years Ilene took antidepressant medication and worked with a therapist to control her "self-destructive behavior." She felt a sense of accomplishment in getting her life under control. Her grades improved, and she completed her degree in marketing. She did not attend her college graduation, nor did she invite either parent to celebrate with her. With her two brothers, she shared a drink in a local pub to mark the occasion of graduating and finding a job. Looking back, she had mixed feelings. On one hand, she sometimes ponders what it would have been like to celebrate with a family. On the other hand, she congratulates herself on avoiding more pain by refusing to try another family celebration.

For four years Ilene was self-sufficient and relatively happy ensconced in the challenges of a career she enjoyed. Then, just before her twenty-fifth birthday, Ilene met Dan. He was three years older than she and more mature than other young men she had dated. Remembering her therapy, she worked hard to establish a relationship with him that was not dependent upon sexuality. With Dan she found a level of intimacy, caring, and companionship she had never before experienced. After several months of dating, the couple began planning their wedding.

Conflict around planning her wedding surprised Ilene. She did not expect her parents' divorce to invade her world once again. She was caught off guard by her mother's insistence that her stepfather be dominant in the wedding. "After all, your father left us. Jack was always there for you, even when you were hell on wheels. What has your father ever done but make your life miserable?" Though not as verbal, her father was equally steadfast with his control of finances. Money given was contingent upon his and his wife's place in the ceremony. After a few weeks, Ilene became depressed and began having nightmares. Afraid that she was making a mistake by marrying, she called off the wedding. One month later, she and Dan announced a small, private wedding. Her parents were invited but seated on opposite sides of the church. None were included in the ceremony. As she recalled these events in therapy, she tearfully spoke of how painful it was to realize she had lost yet another dream—her wedding—to divorce.

As we continued working through Ilene's genogram, similar patterns of grief, loss, depression, and relational disruption emerged at every point in her family development cycle. She began to see how her family's divorce touched every area of her emotional life and how loss and grief provided an overlay for her experience. Her marital life had been lived in fear that Dan would leave her. And, of course, he did. Every celebration–Amy's birth, her brothers' marriages—carried the shadow of family loss. And now she feared for her own future. Could she maintain a marriage? Could she be in a new relationship that did not allow deceit and lies? She knew that people without a family history of divorce were just as likely to fail in marriage, but she still feared she was doomed to repeat her mother's life and that Amy was destined to relive hers. It seemed that the effects of divorce threw a cloud of loss, fear, grief, and anxiety over every family decision and relationship in her life.

As we completed Ilene's study of her family history, she was no longer confused about why she was feeling depressed and afraid. Life was going well. It was going too well, and she was facing another developmental transition that would surely be invaded by her history of divorce grief and loss.

Ilene's case is paradigmatic. It illustrates grief as it reverberates throughout an individual's life cycle and through family systems over generations. It also shows how behavior sciences underestimate grief's long-term effects. Professionals with whom Ilene worked attended to her "oppositional" and "self-destructive behavior." However, therapists did not recognize how deeply divorce loss impacted her family and her life as a developing child, teen, young adult, spouse, and parent.

For children and adults, immediate and long-term problems are more than adjustment reactions to divorce and remarriage. Helping divorced individuals and families adapt to changing life circumstances is a therapeutic necessity and an important focus for pastoral care. However, therapists and carers may be frustrated when critical adjustment tasks are successful and emotional or behavioral symptoms persist, worsen, or recur.

Adjustment problems are easy to see and define. What is not so clear is that many, if not most, immediate and long-term problems in divorced families are directly related to losses of divorce itself. Recovery is not a simple matter of reorganizing life to meet new, specific challenges. Children are affected by multiple waves of delayed emotional and behavioral problems that wash through their lives in cycles of years and decades after parental divorce. This little studied "sleeper effect"[1] produces developmental regression, acting out behavior, depression, and anxiety. Several studies, including one very large British project,[2] conclude that children are likely to carry these divorce symptoms into adult life. Stepfamilies are threatened as they face these complex, emotionally loaded problems. Remarried couples are highly vulnerable to conflict and disintegration when nonbiologically shared children have problems.

Although research has not identified adult "sleeper effects," similar phenomena are easy to observe in counseling. Divorced people, remarried couples, and adult children whose parents divorced often enter therapy and overlook the role divorce losses play in their difficulties. When an astute counselor or pastoral carer explores the impact of divorce on their history of problems, repetitive cycles of grief and loss are usually found painfully close to the surface. Deep psychological undercurrents related to divorce often complicate simple matters of adjustment to new circumstances, role confusion, and normal stressors. It is critical for pastoral carers and counselors to understand the multiple dimensions of divorce grief and how these manifest in cycles that revolve through stepfamily life.

Loss and Grief as Central Analogy

Divorce loss and grief in a family can be compared to a handful of stones tossed into a network of small, interconnecting pools. A series of complex waves quickly spreads across the surface of the water. The largest and most obvious effects are close to the point of impact. But a careful observer will notice that, over time, waves will touch and impact even the most remote part of the network. No part of the system is untouched either in reach or in depth. How much change or damage the waves cause is determined by a variety of factors—how large the stones were, how violently they were thrown, how extensive and deep the pools are, and what mitigating or protective resources were present when the event took place.

---

[1]Judith Wallerstein, *Second Chances: Men, Women and Children a Decade after Divorce* (New York: Houghton-Mifflin Co., 1996); Bray and Kelly, *Stepfamilies*.

[2]B. Rodgers, C. Power, and H. Steven, "Parental Divorce and Adult Psychological Distress: Evidence from a National Cohort: A Research Note," *Journal of Child Psychology and Psychiatry and Allied Disciplines* 38, no. 7 (1997): 867–72.

Because each family and divorce is different, neither the pattern of waves nor their effects will be identical from family to family. Remarkable differences may be obvious. It is equally true that no matter how unique the family, waves of grief will permeate the system, will have their effects, and will be at least partially predictable in how they do that.

By now we know that divorce "waves" are large and destructive for couples and children for at least two years and probably as long as five. We know, for instance, that within two years of divorce, immediate family members are six times more likely to be hospitalized for psychological disorders. Divorced people are twice as likely to become depressed and act out in self-destructive ways, including successful suicide. They are more accident prone, more willing to take unreasonable risks, more susceptible to physical illnesses, and more likely to abuse drugs and alcohol than nondivorced people. Rates of cancer, heart disease, vocational disturbances, and social disruptions are higher among the divorced than among the first-married.[3] Holmes and Rahe,[4] psychologists who studied the effects of life stress, rated divorce along with death of a spouse as the most stressful of all life events.

Parent-child relationships are particularly vulnerable close to the divorce event. In addition to anxiety about custody, child support, and change, parents may be so debilitated by loss, grief, and humiliation that they become ineffective. Children then lose parents who can make the hard decisions about limits, rules, expectations, and consequences. In some cases, adults become so self-absorbed that they either become distant with children or become dependent and over-engaged. Either strategy may soothe the guilt and fear of marital loss, but both blur the emotional boundaries between children and parents. Such parent-child disruptions put children at risk for a constellation of developmental difficulties.[5]

When parents divorce, children's commonly regress emotionally and behaviorally. Many display high levels of anger or destructive behavior. Others will become anxious and preoccupied, socially withdrawn, or excessively dependent. School performance for most will suffer. These are usually seen as symptoms of children adjusting to "a chain of marital

[3]C. Briscoe et al., "Divorce and Psychiatric Disease," *Archives of General Psychiatry* 29 (1973); B. Bloom, S. White, and S. Asher, "Marital Disruption as a Stressor: A Review and Analysis," *Psychological Bulletin* (June 1978).

[4]T. Holmes and R. Rahe, "The Social Readjustment Rating Scale," *Journal of Psychosomatic Reasearch* 11 (1967).

[5]V. Roseby and J. Johnston, "Children of Armageddon: Common Developmental Threats in High Conflict Divorcing Families," *Child and Adolescent Psychiatric Clinics of North America* 7 (1998): 295–309. See also Wallerstein, *Second Chances;* and Bray and Kelly, *Stepfamilies.*

transitions and shifting life experiences."[6] But to see these problems only as transitional is to miss a critical fact: While they are acute markers of change, they are also part of a broader, recurring pattern of grief permanently imbedded in a divorce-affected developmental life cycle.

Popular divorce recovery literature attends well to children's and adults' multiple transitions, adjustments, and acute grief reactions. However, most authors play a variation of a single melody: Divorce grief is a time-limited stage. It will be a central theme for twelve to eighteen months. Self-help literature suggests that the grieving process is predictable and will follow some variation of thanatologist Elisabeth Kübler-Ross's four-stage, death-related model.[7] Worksheets, programs, and books are sold to guide divorcing people through anxiety about their own and their children's reactions. The subtle message of this literature is that divorce grief can be resolved cleanly, clearly, and completely by thoroughly working through each stage of grief. The unspoken promise: Hard work that resolves grief early in the process will preempt later eruptions. If the program is carefully followed, both children and adults will return to pre-divorce levels of functioning with little enduring effect.

A RECAPITULATING THEME

Conceptualizing grief as transition softens a far deeper, soul-piercing reality of persistent loss in divorce. The best grief work done by the most motivated people early in divorce will not keep normal events in the individual and stepfamily life cycle from reactivating grief. The initial tidal wave of emotion may recede in the first year or two of divorce, but the enduring effects of loss will reverberate through parents, children, grandparents, aunts, uncles, and cousins as individual and family developmental mileposts are negotiated. As Ilene's story illustrates, divorce-related family processes will recapitulate in powerful, unexpected ways during times of progress, celebration, and ritual passage. Those who are closest to the impact and most vulnerable to disequilibrium will be forced to revisit and resolve renewed grief.

Several factors predispose stepfamilies to recapitulating grief. First, most couples who remarry do so within one to three years of divorce. This guarantees that most stepfamilies begin their journey with grief about nuclear family loss close to the surface. Newly married couples are faced with the complex task of sorting through the remarriage maze of relationships and

---

[6]E. Hetherington, Tracy Law, and Thomas O'Connor, "Divorce: Challenges, Changes, and New Chances," in *Normal Family Processes*, 2d ed., ed. Froma Walsh (New York: Guilford, 1993), 209.

[7]Elisabeth Kübler-Ross, *On Death and Dying* (New York: Macmillan, 1969; New York: Scribner Classics, 1997).

meanings with their emotional resources compromised by active grief. This begins in the dating process and follows the couple through the wedding and into early family life.

Dating quickly accesses issues of divorce grief. As ex-spouses turn toward new romantic interests, children confront the reality that any hope of their parents' reunion is growing more remote. While they may be excited about Mom's or Dad's new dating life, overt or unconscious protest to their parents' new relationships is almost universal. A child's dissent may be as simple as anxious clinging when Mom is preparing to leave on her date night or an upset stomach that delays Dad in leaving for an evening rendezvous. It may be as complex as cycles of raging tantrums or physical outbursts. Most remarried couples can tell humorous and painful stories about their children's resistant reaction to their budding relationship. Seeing parents bond with new partners is an all-too-real reminder of what was lost. It can recapitulate children's grief and spark a replay of divorce-related symptoms. For emotionally healthy parents, guilt and confusion about their children's divorce losses will augment normal ambivalence about dating, new relationships, and the possibility of remarriage.

Dating adults will confront their own residual grief. This comes in the form of questions about trust, unwillingness to commit to new relationships, and fear of behavior patterns in a dating partner that resemble those of an ex-spouse. Newly single people often try to avoid reminders of their past spouse in a new potential mate. Many take extreme measures to ensure that any romantic interest is as opposite their "ex" as possible. This, of course, is a reactive stance that predisposes more loss. Potentially good relationships may be rejected by hypervigilant sensitivity to first-marriage losses. Disastrous relationships may be exuberantly embraced with naive blindness to how similar the "differences" in their new partner are to characteristics of an "ex" that caused so much pain in their previous marriage. Emotionally healthy people who date long enough to move below the surface of these reactive positions soon find complex patterns of attraction and attachment that are not so easily categorized. These couples eventually recognize that some of the characteristics that delight them about their new love are familiar—they were attracted to them in their previous marriage. Likewise, they will be frightened and irritated by patterns that are equally familiar. This is a normal process, but fuels repetitive themes of anxiety and loss that must once again be "resolved" in the cycle of grief.

At the very least, couples who date seriously and consider remarriage face the painful, personal, and historic reality that love can be lost, confidences can be used against one, and even the most unbeguiling partner can betray. Trusting a new spouse requires that some of divorce's old grief be adequately resolved. At the same time, trusting again demands that betrayal's grief be relived in order to make decisions about a new relationship.

Rituals and celebrations provide unparalleled opportunities to showcase family process. Unresolved issues across generations explode onto the scene at funerals, childbirth, holidays, and weddings in brilliant technicolor fully supported by amazing special effects. In the best of circumstances family rites elicit the words, tears, and hurt feelings of unresolved family anxiety laid bare by transition. When divorced people remarry, high levels of anxiety imbedded in the family system erupt across generational boundaries. Grandparents may spark intergenerational conflict at a wedding by expressing ambivalence about their children's marital choices. Family members who have maintained attachments to an ex-spouse may be reluctant to join in celebrating a new marriage. It is not uncommon for an aunt, an uncle, or even a grandparent to increase their contact with an ex-spouse as a wedding day approaches. At the same time a divorced couple is trying to introduce a new mate into the family system, the system itself resists by holding on to the old one. Divorce grief is activated, anxiety rises, and conflict is inevitable. While anxiety and conflict are usual at first weddings, they touch a far deeper grief for children and couples in a subsequent marriage.

Children often greet a parent's wedding day with excitement about festivities tempered by sadness about the final demise of hope for Mom, Dad, and children living together in one home. Divorce grief recapitulates as parents explain to young children why their father or mother cannot be invited to the wedding and emphasize the "forever" quality of their new marriage. Couples themselves often have reservations about their remarriage that are driven by the residue of previous loss. For the divorced, remarriage is a delicate hope laced with conscious and unconscious ambivalence expressed verbally and nonverbally throughout the intergenerational family system. It is far too easy to lose the redemptive and hopeful spirit of remarriage in this morass of recapitulated grief.

Divorce loss and grief is a durable fixture of stepfamily life. For successful stepfamilies, it is managed well, incrementally recedes, and then lies in remission, awaiting times of significant stress or developmental transition. Recapitulating grief in remarriage binds itself to the multiple transitions of becoming a new family and generates a storm of new "waves." The first two years of remarried life hold the most intense crises, the most clearly defined developmental transitions, and the most poignant opportunities for relived grief. It is during this period that stepfamilies are most likely to disintegrate.

As Ilene's case demonstrates, recapitulating grief will have particular power early in marriage while a new stepfamily negotiates rules, boundaries, roles, and relationships. However, any transition at any time in the stepfamily life cycle will recall the loss of divorce and produce emotional and behavioral symptoms. Whether these are mild or severe will depend on how well the family has developed internal resources, the psychological health of individual family members, the family's network of support, and the level of external pressure on the family (i.e., financial distress, vocational dissatisfaction, cultural oppression, etc.). Holiday seasons and religious celebrations ritualize family connections. Nuclear family nostalgia is inflated, and relational loss is amplified. During these times, stepfamilies are vulnerable to exquisite episodes of restated grief. Church members will be close to, and sometimes a part of, behavioral and emotional fallout. It is tempting for church leaders to blame symptomatic eruptions on something easy to manage, such as temporary transitional issues, dysfunctional family processes, or a troublesome family member. However, when pastoral leaders, therapists, and carers dismiss these painful episodes as "normal" stepfamily process or label family members with psychological diagnoses, they miss opportunities to initiate the conversations that lead to critical dialogue and praxis.

Stepfamilies that thrive are experts at modulating grief. They learn how to bring it to conscious attention and carefully hold it in the context of their new relationships. Unfortunately, grief that is unnamed or cloaked in a mantle of "stepfamily adjustment" will dismember many families before they have a chance to succeed. Broken stepfamilies find slim comfort in knowing that they are the majority. After all, most stepfamilies fail. For them, this means only that grief is compounded. Sensitive pastoral carers will not be distracted by easy definitions of stepfamily processes or quick fixes for their problems. Instead, they will attend to the complex interactions between transition, adjustment, and grief and take this carefully into empowering, transforming conversations with stepfamilies.

MNEMONIC LOSS IN STEPFAMILY EXPERIENCE

Pastoral care attends to persons in their concrete, embodied experience. One way humans make sense of experience is by organizing it and symbolizing it through a framework of meaning-making narratives that have continuity across generations. By identifying with these stories, we "remember" past generations and catch the thread of common meaning, which attaches us in culturally specific ways to human community. Stepfamilies are a "problem" because they do not fit easily into the cultural and religious narrative. When we think of "family," we unconsciously turn to our transgenerational cultural memory, which is embodied in timeless stories that tell us what families are like and what families are supposed to be. Individual family stories find meaning in how they fit and connect with this communally shared reality.

Except in negative ways, stepfamily stories do not fit this embodied memory. They are alienated from dominant cultural and religious understandings of "family." Those who observe stepfamilies through this deeply imbedded, unconscious frame either will see an alien life form with which they have no shared heritage or will miss stepfamily differences and insist that they behave as they "should"—as nuclear families. Part of stepfamily grief is a lost common connection with the cultural and religious family narrative. They do not share in the collective memory and are themselves not "remembered" in any positive sense. This loss is intense when it crystalizes in intimate relationships or power-laden contexts of politics, education, business, congregational ministry, and pastoral care.

Divorce subverts a family's story from the broader cultural and multi-generational narrative, but it also creates a more personal loss. Marital dissolution ruptures the relational context that gives continuity to how important life events are interpreted and remembered. The family's specific story of meaning and personal connection is lost or forever changed. Without a shared collective value, memories are altered; family stories are forgotten because there is no longer a unified context that draws meaning from them, contains them, or safeguards them from loss. History is revised in the light of a failed marriage. Grief escalates, and alienation is profound. This loss recirculates when divorced couples remarry. Successful stepfamilies will reorganize important, unifying nuclear-family memories in service of the new couple and the stepfamily.

Newly married stepfamilies will walk away from their wedding ceremony steeped in loss and mnemonic alienation. As a new family, their journey takes them into a land of psychological and spiritual homelessness. There they are pressed either to create a new narrative memory bound to the old only by fragments of tattered flesh or to make themselves fit into family visions consistent with the dominant cultural story. The former is very hard, the latter impossible and damaging.

It is little wonder that divorced and remarried adults and their children feel disoriented and separated from their own pasts, their cultural present, and their individual family future. They must write a new story in a vacuum devoid of guiding cultural or religious narratives. Without these broader connections, new stories become well-kept secrets. Joys are hidden because of their shameful origins, and pain is masked to cover the power of dark, forbidding undercurrents of loss. The whole, embodied truth of stepfamily life is not easily told. It is not easily heard and is easily misunderstood.

Against the background of guiding cultural and religious narratives in which stepfamilies only marginally share, judgment is quick and sure. Effective pastoral care must begin in careful, respectful listening that empowers divorced and remarried people to connect their stories with gospel narratives and life in the body of Christ.

SIN AND TRAGEDY: EMBODIED STORIES OF GRIEF

Loss is one critical story that groans unceasingly from the depths of stepfamily experience. It is permanent and will recycle throughout stepfamily development. Its symptoms will affect the edges of congregational life and at times erupt acutely at its center. Effective carers will have ears tuned to hear this subjugated story, which lies just below the surface of emotionally charged stepfamily problems.

Recycling grief is central to stepfamily pain. It is also the place where religious care has the most to offer. Grief, after all, is not just behavioral. It is also spiritual. Recovery is more than surviving transitions, managing behavioral problems, and living to see less pain at the end of a two-year period than was there at the beginning. Grief recovery starts with an invitation to be a part of a storied community of faith that empowers wounded people to tell the truth. Healing begins when suppressed stepfamily stories find acceptance and common connection with enduring religious narratives rooted not in perfect outcomes, but in loss that meets redemption and grief that is integrated into embodied resurrection. This requires a context that values truth and can lovingly hold intense feelings of loss lived, relived, and then lived again. Pastoral care must participate in truth-telling and constructing new redemptive stories for stepfamilies. To do this, congregational carers must create safe environments where the fullness of stepfamily stories can be told. They must then help divorced and remarried families articulate the pathos of their loss in a way that connects them with the faith community's redemptive narrative. Sin and tragedy are dual themes closely connected to central Christian narratives. These can give voice to recycling grief. When the truth is told by divorced families, two related sets of affective vectors capture their emotional life: guilt and remorse, hopeless sorrow and helpless rage. These are recycled through divorce recovery, single-parenthood, and stepfamily development. Together, they embody both sin and tragedy.

Every divorce is a result of sin played out in a marital relationship. Broken promises, shattered covenants, irreconcilable differences, unwillingness to change, abuse, neglect, self-serving isolation—names cease to matter. Divorce, as Jesus noted, does not happen without a root fixed solidly in sin. The emotional results of sin revolve through divorced persons' lives in shifting shades of guilt, remorse, and denial. In all except the most callous people, themes of personal responsibility for marital failure play a large role in divorce stories. Some of these are well deserved, others less. However, even those who suffer divorce because of others' actions will carry a weight of guilt and remorse because of their own flaws, personalities, or perceived shortcomings. When guilt about sin is not resolved, it becomes bondage that handicaps a redemptive future. It undercuts hope, contaminates new covenants, and adds excessive power to recycling grief in stepfamily life.

Naming guilt and remorse is a task that is shared between the community of faith and persons who have been divorced. The community must help some people take responsibility for destructive relational attitudes and behavior they have never before faced. Others, such as abused or abandoned spouses and children, call for the faithful community to temper inappropriate ideas of personal guilt with images of suffering and tragic loss. Appropriately naming sin and its loss-laden results helps a family construct a new story that balances just guilt with transforming remorse. Here, sin can be connected to God's promise of forgiveness and release from the bondage of guilt.

Pastoral care in counseling, preaching, and teaching must empower persons in divorced families to integrate their sin against a former marriage into their family story. This is a difficult private and public conversation. It must somehow connect realistic confession to God's forgiveness and atonement through the community's life, symbols, and rituals. In the Christian community, the question of sin, guilt, and forgiveness calls for the gospel answer of baptism and new life in Christ. The story of individual sin and forgiveness, including divorce, finds its resolution in the narrative of God's renewing forgiveness symbolized in Christ's death and resurrection. This is ritualized in baptism, which promises release from old guilt and a covenant bound within the faithful community to live in new ways. To sin, die, and rise to new life is a central healing metaphor for those who remarry and begin again in stepfamilies.

Guilty remorse fused to a stepfamily's recapitulating grief finds its relief in God's grace. Congregational care must remind divorced Christians of God's grace, which is present in their baptism. It is embodied forgiveness. At the same time, care must help divorced persons reinterpret their baptismal vow to include accountability for transformed life in Christ that insists they keep new promises, abandon deceit in marriage, and continue discipleship. Care that recalls baptism will empower new dimensions to an old family story of divorce.

Divorce grief is not only about sin. It also expresses a deep theme of tragedy embodied in hopeless sorrow and helpless rage. Divorce creates victims of injustice. First, divorces are rarely mutual. One person can foist

an unwanted divorce on another. One spouse can deceive the other or abandon one who does not deserve it. Spouse abuse leaves no humane choice—
leave or die. Children have no choice at all. Beyond the personal, divorce
creates a context of social injustice. He (rarely she) who has the most money
to hire the best lawyers wins the prize in the divorce race. Women and
children are cast into poverty. Social forces and judicial policy beyond any
individual's control now determine the form, worth, and activities of family life. Losses are immense and reflect tragic injustice that far transcends
the result of individual sin. All divorce stories contain overtones of rage and
sorrow that accompany tragedy.

The question of sin finds its answer in God's forgiveness. Tragedy looks
to God's presence in compassionate love with those who suffer. Loss and
lament followed by a promise of restoration is a cycle that revolves endlessly
through scriptural tradition and the faithful community's narrative. God
knows those who suffer and enters their grief with them. God promises
restoration to those who suffer irreparable loss. Promise is fulfilled by a
covenant community that immerses itself in others' suffering and then stands
with the oppressed to express God's defiance of injustice. This is the history
of God's people, which is most clearly expressed in the Christian symbol of
communion.

In Christ's broken body and shed blood, God is immersed in human
tragedy and suffering. Resurrection enacts God's defiant refusal to allow sin
or cultural, religious, and political power to strip away the hope, meaning,
and redemptive purposes of Jesus' life and ministry. In communion, the
Lord's supper, the Christian community joins with a God who is immersed
in human pain and suffering. We symbolize our connection to Jesus, who
is our "brother in suffering."[8] Christ's followers, who have experienced God's
compassionate love, stand together at the banquet table and symbolize union
in broken humanity. In the faithful communion of the saints, those broken
by tragedy find God's compassionate presence. It is God, and God embodied in this community, who will stand with them and defy the powers that
would overwhelm them and relegate them to hopeless sorrow and helpless
rage.

Divorced and remarried people are included in the communion narrative through two distinct motions. Movement inward draws suffering people
into the community and to communion. For the church, this means that
divorce sorrow must be heard, be embraced, and become part of the
congregation's story. The community can only embody God's presence with
suffering divorced people by empathic immersion. "Their" pain must

---

[8]Jurgen Moltmann, *Jesus Christ for Today's World* (Minneapolis, Minn: Fortress Press, 1994), 3.

become "our" pain; their story of tragic suffering becomes part of our story together. Compassionate pastoral care empowers the church to engage families at the point of their deepest sorrow and then draws them to safety, where they can tell the truth with people who understand as God understands. This kind of safety empowers people wounded by tragedy to risk healing communion.

Communion also symbolizes movement outward. Compassionate pastoral care stands in defiant resistance to the injustices inherent in divorce that continue to wound single-parent families and stepfamilies throughout their lives. This defiance is both public and private. As God met crucifixion with resurrection, the community of the risen Christ meets divorce tragedy with concrete action that enlivens restoration hope through care for individual families and a public voice raised against divorce-related social injustice. Suffering and death shout for resurrection and a living God who forces the powers of torment to retreat and makes those who are tortured well again.[9]

In communion, at the intersection of divorce's story and faith's narrative, hope erupts. Cycles of tragedy are broken, and families held hostage by hopeless sorrow and helpless rage are released.

GRIEF, LOSS, AND HUMAN WHOLENESS

Pastoral care is about finding connections to human wholeness in the face of pain, fragmentation, and loss. This is a story with universal dimensions. Humanity's story is one of creation, loss, and grief to which God responds with redemptive action. God meets people who have lost their place in dominant religious and cultural narratives. Through God's action, an alienated, broken community finds a new story that makes sense of their experience, promises healing from grief, and restores lost identity. This cycle permeates the biblical narrative and finds complete expression in Christ.

Hope for remarried families is in congregational care that recognizes their loss and grief as part of the universal human narrative of longing for new beginnings and fresh starts. This is voiced by stories of restoration and God's good news of deliverance:

> The Spirit of the Lord GOD is upon me,
> because the LORD has anointed me;
> he has sent me to bring good news to the oppressed,
> to bind up the brokenhearted,
> to proclaim liberty to the captives,
> and release to the prisoners;

---

[9]Moltmann, *Jesus Christ*, 13.

to proclaim the year of the LORD's favor,
    and the day of vengeance of our God;
    to comfort all who mourn;
to provide for those who mourn in Zion—
    to give them a garland instead of ashes,
the oil of gladness instead of mourning,
    the mantle of praise instead of a faint spirit.
They will be called oaks of righteousness,
    the planting of the LORD, to display his glory.
They shall build up the ancient ruins,
    they shall raise up the former devastations;
they shall repair the ruined cities,
    the devastations of many generations.
                                    (Isaiah 61:1–4)

Stepfamily hope is a story beginning in loss, lived in recapitulating loss, and resting in identification and solidarity with God's restoration.

Chapter 5
Marginal (Re)Marriage

Stepfamilies are created when once-married people with children from former marriages decide to try again. For most, this decision is filled with hope. Most know remarriage will be hard. Many know it will be more complicated than their first marriage. But nearly all couples expect that they will beat the odds with a happy marriage and an effective stepfamily.

Stepfamily cohesion is built on a strong couple relationship. When stepfamilies fail, it is because the couple relationship fails. All good marriages require commitment and hard work, but remarried couples must negotiate a morass of complicated relationships, divided loyalties, stressors, and emotional land mines before they find marital satisfaction. Larry and Sharon illustrate how confusing and difficult this can be for remarried couples.

> Larry Willis had been divorced six months when he met Sharon Brooks. His wife, Pam, had left him and his two young children for another man. Since he did not want divorce, he contested every part of the process. After fighting for a full year, Larry was tired of conflict. He severed all contact with Pam, took his bills, daughter, and son and moved across the country for a new life close to his boyhood home. With his father's help, he found a job managing a division of a large construction company. The job paid well, had regular work hours, and allowed him reasonable time with ten-year-old Mary and twelve-year-old Drew. He worked hard to be a good single parent. His children were entirely dependent upon him. They had no contact with their mother apart from annual summer visitation. Larry felt this was only right. He resented his children's spending any time with a woman who could foment such immense betrayal.

Sharon had been divorced for nearly five years when she met Larry. Her first marriage had been emotionally abusive. Her husband, Pete, was demanding and prone to explosive, angry episodes. Though he never physically harmed either her or her two sons, he did occasionally break furniture and damage drywall. She suspected that he drank excessively near the end of their marriage. Just after her fifteenth wedding anniversary, something "just broke" inside her. She realized she was thirty-nine years old and had two children who were growing fast. One was in middle school, the other in elementary school. She did not want to live in constant fear of her husband's outrageous behavior. One Friday in January, she told her husband she would no longer tolerate his abuse. She demanded he begin counseling with her to change their marriage, or he would have to leave. Pete laughed at her, informed her that she could never make it on her own, and left. Within the week Sharon found employment at a local construction office and filed for divorce. Her contact with Pete was limited to his occasional visits to see his sons. He refused regular visitation, preferring instead to "drop over" at his convenience or invite his sons to his new home for special occasions.

Larry and Sharon met at work. Larry was attracted to Sharon, who was "good-looking" and "seemed to be able to run the whole business single-handed." He liked her easy smile, her basic cheerfulness, and her straightforward, no-nonsense approach to problems. Sharon was wary of men. She responded to most advances with, "I don't date. I've got enough on my mind with two kids without making things worse with a man." This discouraged most from asking again. She knew Larry liked her and appreciated that he did not push or ask her out. Later Larry remembered this as his heartfelt vow never to trust a woman again and never to remarry. Sharon saw Larry as a "sweet, gentle man" to whom she could easily talk. He lived out some "firm Christian values" that had been missing with her first husband. After two months of daily contact, Sharon asked Larry, "Why don't you take me out?" Larry remembered laughing and replying, "Sure, I'll put that on my to-do list for tomorrow." The following day, the couple scheduled their first date.

Eight months later, Larry and Sharon were at a crossroads. They cared for each other deeply, had become sexually involved, and had grown to know each other's children. They now had common friends, church connections, and some shared recreational interests. Though they had talked of marriage, they were both ambivalent because of past abuse and betrayal. However, after several weeks of anxious discussion, they began to plan their wedding.

Sharon's children were not enthusiastic about her plans to remarry. Eight-year-old Jon regressed to clinging dependency, while fifteen-year-old

Bryan said simply, "He's not going to tell me what to do." Larry's twelve-year-old son, Drew, said nothing in response to his plans to remarry. Ten-year-old Mary was interested in the details of the wedding, but also began to ruminate and worry about her mother's safety and well-being. In late August, after dating just over a year, the couple married.

The wedding itself was uneventful. There were a few disruptions by children who were angry about not getting their way, and one instance where Mary cried because she missed her mother. Both Larry and Sharon looked back fondly on their brief honeymoon in the mountains. They appreciated friends who kept their children so they could have a weekend alone.

Moving two families into one home was a cascade of disaster. Larry had purchased a moderately sized house when he moved into the area. Sharon had rented an apartment. Since the couple could not afford to purchase a larger home together, they moved into Larry's three-bedroom house. Twelve-year-old Drew was required to share his room with eight-year-old Jon. Drew complained about having a "snot-nosed mama's boy" living with him. He didn't want "baby toys" cluttering his room. Jon refused to sleep in his new room and told Sharon that Drew had threatened to scare him in the middle of the night. He wanted to move back to their apartment. No amount of consoling would soothe Jon into sleeping in "Drew's room." Bryan was given a small alcove that Larry had converted into a tiny fourth bedroom. Mary kept her original bedroom. Drew demanded that if she got to keep her own room, so should he.

Larry and Sharon disagreed about how to resolve this problem. Their first night together, the couple faced Jon's tears and anxiety. Over Larry's protests, Sharon invited Jon into their new king-size bed. Her stand was: Either Jon would sleep with her in their bedroom, or she would sleep on the couch with Jon. Three weeks later, Jon was still in their bed. Both Jon and Drew were happy with this arrangement. Neither Larry nor Sharon felt it was safe to talk about the problem.

Apart from bedroom arrangements, the couple faced other space problems. There was not enough room for everyone's belongings. Rather than ask the children to give up toys, creative storage was arranged. Larry and Sharon sorted clothes and utensils, giving away what was not needed or was impossible to store. Space and ownership sparked the couple's first major conflict. Before moving, Larry had sold the furniture from his first marriage. He later financed new furniture at great expense. Most of Sharon's furniture had been given to her by her parents. She was unwilling to part with family heirlooms. Larry soon discovered the "downside" to what had attracted him to Sharon—her no-nonsense manner and her ability to make decisions and make them stick. Sharon discovered that behind Larry's good-natured cheerfulness was a "hardheaded" side that didn't always listen to "good sense." After several weeks of conflict, the couple placed several heirlooms in storage alongside some of Larry's new furniture. They would figure out what to do with it later.

Less than a month after the wedding, Sharon caught Bryan sneaking out of the house. His room was separated from the other bedrooms, and he easily climbed out a window without being noticed. When mother and son's confrontation became noisy and included profanity, Larry was pulled into the fray. He informed Bryan that he would not tolerate anyone's speaking in this way to his wife and told him to go to his room. Amid invectives, Bryan shouted that Larry had no right to tell him what to do and ran out the door. Larry and Sharon spent a sleepless night awaiting Bryan's return at 4:00 a.m. It was clear he had been drinking.

In the following months, the couple tried to resolve child-related problems. Larry bolted Bryan's window shut, and Sharon tried to enforce limits with him. This was unsuccessful. Most nights, Sharon stayed awake listening for Bryan's departure. She was irritable most days. Her work and her marriage were suffering. When Sharon asked Pete for help, he laughed and commented, "You made this bed, now sleep in it." The couple made some progress with Jon and Drew. One day when the boys were playing well together, Sharon asked Drew if he minded if Jon moved back into his room. Drew agreed. However, on succeeding nights, Jon protested leaving his mother's bed. Some nights Sharon insisted he sleep in his own bed. When she lacked the energy to persevere, Jon rejoined his mother in her marital bed. Although angry, Larry did not resist these semi-regular intrusions.

Nine months into their marriage, Larry and Sharon faced a relationship-threatening problem. Bryan was uncontrollable. He was sneaking out most weekend nights and coming home drunk. He was not attending school and was unaccounted for during the day. Every attempt to confront his behavior met violent defiance. Family counseling was initiated, but Brian was too large to force physically into attendance. They ended their contract with the therapist after three visits. They could not get Bryan there, and the counselor's advice seemed to have no effect. This was compounded when Bryan's school principal called Sharon and told her she was responsible for Bryan's behavior. She must bring him into immediate compliance or face an investigation by Child Protective Services. Sharon confronted Bryan and demanded that he follow the household rules, or she would call the police. Bryan left, stayed out all night, and arrived home the next morning drunk. Larry "blew up" and told him that he was no longer welcome in his home. He would have to find someplace else to live. Sharon was dumbstruck. To protect her son, she drove him to an uncle's house in a neighboring town where he could stay while she "sorted things out." She was so hurt and angry about Larry's ultimatum that she returned to tell him their marriage was over. After talking with her pastor, Sharon agreed to meet with a pastoral counselor before making a final decision. Larry agreed to begin therapy with her.

In the first few sessions, both Larry and Sharon voiced their frustration, anger, and disappointment. Larry told Sharon how angry he was that none of what he expected in marriage had happened. Their time alone had ended when the couple moved in together. There were no more nights out and little time at home together. Larry was particularly angry that Sharon was unavailable for sex. This was compounded by his feeling that Jon's and Bryan's problems had invaded their bedroom. Their door was open to be sure Bryan did not sneak out, and Jon was a frequent visitor. Larry felt their entire life was consumed by children's problems, problem children, and arguments about house rules. He loved Sharon but was burned out and discouraged.

Sharon shared her own pain. She too had expected a close marital relationship with plentiful sex. She was hurt that Larry did not understand Jon's insecurities and felt he had been callous in letting Drew get away with threatening Jon. As for Bryan, she could have used some support, not just anger and blame. She felt unbearable pain watching her oldest child fall apart and replicate his father. Larry had been insensitive and unsupportive. He did not recognize how hard she worked to fit into his expectations and his house. She had tried to make a good home for Mary and Drew, even though they showed her no appreciation. Larry had made no such effort with her children. He had befriended them while he and Sharon were dating, but when the children failed to respond to his idea of fatherhood, he gave up. That was not fair. She now wondered if she had married another self-absorbed man, like Pete, who did not care for her, understand her, or want to work for a marriage.

Listening to the couple's story, the therapist reflected that both felt alone and unsupported. They seemed to have few community, religious, or family resources to help them through the most stressful and difficult time of their lives.

Cohesion, Relationship Development, and Remarriage

Larry and Sharon's story is not unique. Though not all stepfamilies have problems this intense, their case illustrates a problem that is almost universal for remarried couples. Stepfamilies have trouble with cohesion, the emotional-relational "glue" that holds families together. In stepfamilies, this is often weak or uneven. When cohesion is poor, families develop relational symptoms and individuals suffer problems in living.

In traditional families, cohesion begins when unattached young adults marry and create a firm marital-sexual bond. When the family expands through childbirth, the marital bond extends to the couple's children. Parent-child attachment and nurturing the young become primary purposes for the couple. Children become bonded to parents and to one another, and a family becomes "we."

This bonding process is impossible for stepfamilies. First, couples enter marriage with an inherently compromised couple system. Marital-sexual bonding is undermined by past losses, poor social support, and a complex, ready-made family. Second, biological ties that unite parents and ground parent-child bonding are absent between the remarried couple and step-related family members. A stepparent-stepchild bond is not emotionally or legally equal to a parent-child bond. Issues of fidelity, trust, loyalty, and responsibility permeate these relationships and affect couple attachment. Finally, remarried couples and their children do not receive the same quantity or quality of acceptance and advocacy that nuclear families do from extended family and the community.

Remarriage and stepfamily attachment must wind their way through the residue of past relational carnage and the everyday vicissitudes of complex stepfamily living. In hearing remarriage stories, pastoral carers must listen for themes of attachment and loss, cohesion, and relationship development. These will be expressed in the couple relationship, parent-child relationship, stepparent-child relationship, and sibling-stepsibling relationship.

ATTACHMENT AND MARITAL DEVELOPMENT

Family researcher Lyman Wynne[1] suggests that marital relationships progress through four critical processes of growth:

- Attachment and caregiving through complementary affectional bonding
- Communicating, or learning to share attention and exchange meanings and messages
- Joint problem solving and sharing tasks, interests, and activities
- Mutuality, which includes developing patterns of relational renewal and reengagement

---

[1] Lyman Wynne, "The Epigenesis of Relational Systems: A Model for Understanding Family Development," *Family Process* 23 (1984): 297–318.

One additional phase, intimacy, is possible when a couple gains intimate knowledge of each other's needs and experiences through mutuality.

For Wynne, these processes are sequential and rest on an epigenetic principle: The interchanges of each developmental phase build on the outcomes of earlier transactions. If there are problems, distortions, or omissions at any given developmental phase, all subsequent stages will be altered. Each phase has its own effect on marital quality, but establishing a complementary affectional bond is critical. It is this shared attachment that holds the couple together as they face life's difficulties and negotiate communication, problem solving, and mutuality.

There are few exceptions to the rule that successful marriage is dependent on an effective marital-sexual bond. In our culture this attachment tends to "take hold all at once, in full strength."[2] When it happens, the couple will acknowledge and symbolize the central importance of their relationship in exclusive ways, not the least of which is their sexual connection. Daily life may include other attachments and affiliations, but bonded couples will find their primary source of affection and care in each other. The mere physical proximity of their partner will provide comfort. Observe newly bonded couples: They will crave mutual contact, prioritize time for each other, and insist on mutual accessibility. Most often, this will be expressed through a sense of sexual urgency, which affirms mutual emotional and physical availability. In times of distress, they will seek out their partner as a way to diminish anxiety. If access is limited or threatened, they will experience discomfort and loneliness. Attachment behavior, such as clinging demands, jealousy, or emotional distancing, will erupt if one partner finds the other affectively, sexually, or physically absent. Attached couples are not likely to be complacent about days or weeks apart without some definite plan for reestablishing contact.

Marital-sexual attachment takes place early and quickly in the couple's relationship. It does not seem to gain strength with time. In American culture, early attachment takes place mostly in dating rituals and is consummated in the marital covenant. In good long-term relationships, bonding is maintained over time, increases in constancy, and becomes highly resilient. This happens through unconscious and primal processes. Marital attachment touches a deep need that speaks to our fundamental dependency on others. Pastoral theologian James Ashbrook notes that we:

> ...live only as we are connected to that which is other than ourselves. From the umbilical cord that connects the fetus at the navel

---

[2]Robert Weiss, "Attachment in Adult Life," in *The Place of Attachment in Human Behavior,* ed. C. Parkes and J. Stevenson-Hinde (New York: Basic Books, 1982), 179.

with the mother's placenta, to the astronaut's lifeline supplying oxygen and communication while outside the spacecraft, to the spiritual "tie that binds our hearts in…love," we live only to the degree that our supply lines are working properly.[3]

Bonding in marriage provides this kind of primary supply line for emotional protection, security, and relational nutrients needed for marital growth. However, budding attachment constancy is fragile. It is easily interrupted by circumstances that undercut a couple's mutual contact or impede their attachment activity. Stillborn attachment predisposes couples to marital failure.

Remarried couples are capable of good marital-sexual bonding. Those able to nurture attachment during the stress of early remarriage reap marital satisfaction equal to that of first-married couples. Some studies suggest that successful remarried couples actually experience higher levels of marital satisfaction.[4] However, people who remarry with children are at an immediate disadvantage. They instantly face the turbulent early years of stepfamily life and must quickly excel in out-of-phase skills (communication and problem solving) in order to negotiate the critical tasks inherent in remarried life. Pastoral carers must attend to several critical issues that undermine marital-sexual bonding and the relationship development cycle.

Inherently Compromised Couples

Cultural and historic memories of marriage carry specific expectations for couple pairing. In our culture, a man and woman find adequate reason to leave behind the trappings of adolescence or the freedom of singlehood, forsake all others, and then join together for a generative life in common. This decision is based in attraction and affection. It is enacted through public announcement of engagement, some form of marital preparation, and a marriage ritual. The couple is confirmed by immediate and extended kin, the community of faith, and friends. This diverse community sends the couple, amid snickers about sexuality, to their marital bed. A marital-sexual bond is expected to solidify during the isolation of a honeymoon and then be in place when the couple emerges, ready to face the challenges of a family. This cultural promise for marriage is unavailable to many couples, but it is impossible for remarrying couples.

[3]James Ashbrook, *Minding the Soul* (Minneapolis: Augsburg-Fortress Press, 1995), 15.
[4]Elizabeth Vemer et al., "Marital Satisfaction in Remarriage: A Meta-analysis," *Journal of Marriage and Family Therapy* 51 (1989): 713–25.

Insufficient Ritual and Symbol

Weddings are rituals of separation and reconnection that are deeply rooted in cultural and religious tradition. Anderson and Fite[5] suggest that marriage rites are liminal events that mark a significant transition of identity, role, and meaning. They provide a structure for marriage preparation and help couples through the stress of changing status. As a symbolic totality, a wedding is meant to ritualize a forming marital bond and the community's support for the couple. Remarrying couples begin their life nurtured only by fragments of supporting ritual. Most suffer from inadequate preparation. Shame, anxiety about resurfacing grief, fear of institutional disapproval, and dread of discovering more unpleasant divorce issues to resolve discourage some couples from seeking premarital counseling. Others unwisely rely on what they have learned from past experience and divorce recovery. They undermine preparation by discounting what it can offer persons who have been married. Many rightly recognize that most pastors and counselors are not trained to help them, and so they begin remarried life bereft of support from any positive ritual of preparation.

The stabilizing benefit of strong ritual is further weakened by attitudes about remarriage ceremonies. These are, after all, culturally suspect marriages. In popular wisdom, people who divorce are wounded and carry cartloads of unresolved pathology that no amount of therapy or premarital counseling can soften. Two-time and three-time "losers" are even more suspect. A muted celebration half-hidden from view is the appropriate posture for remarriage. To do more is to risk judgment of being presumptuous or reaching for soap-opera theatrics.

Family and friendship factors also complicate wedding rituals. Most remarrying couples do not ask for help in paying for a second celebration, and few parents feel the need to offer support to children "the second time around." After all, their children are not leaving the nest to establish another home. Instead, they are moving from an ambiguous not-really-single, divorced state that includes another (if transitory) home into a muddle of step-relationships without clear boundaries or family ties. Parents, sisters, brothers, and friends of the remarrying couple may be ambivalent about celebrating a new marriage. Many will be caught in conflicting loyalties with ex-spouses that affect their ability to rejoice fully with the new couple. Children are involuntarily participants and are well known for their ability to proclaim their distress clearly, loudly, and with vigor as the wedding day

---

[5]Herbert Anderson and Cotton Fite, *Becoming Married* (Louisville: Westminster Press, 1993), 68–70.

approaches. Their dream of parental reconciliation, after all, ends with their parent's new vows. Children with less permission for self-expression (or whose personalities are less dramatic) may become depressed, withdrawn, or angry.

From multiple sources, the message to remarrying couples is that their commitment is not as valid or worthy as a first marriage. This explains why family investment, community involvement, and celebration are so easily withheld. Remarrying couples carefully invite only those who are certain not to voice judgment to a toned-down, often inexpensive ceremony. For good reason, couples feel isolated and convinced that they are alone in their stepfamily journey. Often, this foreshadows how little support they will have in the future.

Without adequate guidance from religious tradition or cultural wisdom, remarrying couples struggle to manage rites and rituals of marriage. Should the same vows broken by divorce be made to another spouse? How much ceremony and celebration should be planned? Too little diminishes the symbol of marital commitment, and too much reaps judgment. Forty-six-year-old Carol had just announced to her best friend her plans for remarriage. As the two were sharing their joy about this development, her friend asked who was organizing her wedding, who would be in the wedding party, what attendants would wear, and where she was registered for gifts. Carol admitted being utterly confused.

> I'm getting *remarried.* I did all of that for my first. What "wedding party?" This is not going to be a big deal. The only people who will be there will be the two of us, our kids, and a few close friends. I don't want a big public display, and we simply don't have the money for more. Registered? You mean like at Dillard's? I thought gifts were only for first marriages. How do I accept gifts from the same people who gave them to me the first time around?

Her response characterizes popular opinion about remarriage, illustrates lack of guidance for a ritual of remarriage, and highlights the thinly veiled layer of shame that lurks just below the surface at most second weddings.

In their book *Promising Again,* Herbert Anderson, David Hogue, and Marie McCarthy express hope that the religious community will encourage a sense of communal reality for a remarrying couple through careful attention to ritual and ceremony. Marital preparation and weddings can be a time to "bring together a wonderfully diverse multitude made up of the communities in which the couple belong. The gathering of all these supportive communities signals the awareness of, and the need for, the support of many others who *promised again* along with the marrying couple."[6] Furthermore, remarrying couples should be encouraged to see their marriage as a parable of human finitude and imperfection. This deserves the most complete ceremony and celebration possible, including space for children and others to grieve what is irreparably lost. A remarriage ceremony should express fully the humanity of divorced people by accomplishing several ends. First, it should help prepare remarrying couples for the stress and reality of new marriage in complex circumstances. Second, it must honor the feelings of those who cannot participate in the ceremony for personal or theological reasons. Finally, it must symbolize God's forgiveness, our human reliance on God's creative activity in making new promises, and the couple's dependence on God to guarantee their promise to each other and family in the face of human frailty.

Unfortunately, this hopeful vision fails to extend to pastoral guides for wedding ceremonies. Pastors and remarrying couples are left on their own to create the rituals and symbols necessary to undergird chaotic transitions into newly remarried life. Often these are insufficient to anchor couples as they face stepfamily life and its inherent erosion of marital attachment.

INTENSE PARENT-CHILD ALLIANCES

Stepfamily life begins in a context of biological "mini-families,"[7] which predate and emotionally precede a couple's voluntary relationship. Larry and Sharon Willis' story shows how emotionally intense parent-child alliances impact couple bonding. Sharon and her children had always been close. That fact sustained her family through a traumatic divorce and years of difficult single-parenting. Larry's connection with his children was intensified by his divorce. He had been an active parent, but suddenly losing his wife catapulted him into a dependent emotional relationship with his children. In the pain of his marital abandonment, he moved to a region far from his children's nuclear home. While this relieved the daily ache of abandonment for him and his children, it augmented their mutual dependency and tight emotional bond.

Larry and Sharon's post-divorce relational tactics had helped them adapt to single-parent living and provided security for their children. However, tightly bonded parent-child alliances were not easily relinquished at the altar of remarriage. Like other newlyweds, they needed solitude, time alone

---

[6]Herbert Anderson, David Hogue, and Marie McCarthy, *Promising Again* (Louisville: Westminster John Knox Press, 1995), 115.

[7]Jamie Keshet, "From separation to stepfamily: A subsystem analysis," *Journal of Family Issues* 1 (1980): 517–32.

for sexual spontaneity, and space away from children to learn to argue and negotiate. These needs posed a clear threat to primitive, unilateral, biological parent-child bonds. When the couple tried to find space for couple development, they immediately faced intense reactions within parent-child relationships. Marriage, for them, was more than a transition into a new phase of life or a path to adulthood and generativity. Instead, it was a personal-relational transition that interrupted the child-rearing stage of adulthood.

Both Larry and Sharon were attached to children independent of their marriage. When they joined families, loyalties became confused. Unconscious filial allegiance pushed both to react in ways that undermined their marriage and confirmed their primary loyalty to their children. Sharon sacrificed marital satisfaction for her son's comfort. Space and time for the couple's budding sexual bond was sacrificed to Jon's need for soothing attachment to his mother. On the other hand, Larry risked his attachment with Sharon when he failed to set limits with Drew. By protecting Drew from invasion by a stepbrother, he made a firm parent-child statement: Drew's needs took priority over his own, over Sharon's, and over Jon's. Though Larry blamed Sharon for her children's problems, his own collusion with Drew participated equally in Jon's presence in their marital bed. Furthermore, Sharon was left alone to carry the full weight of Bryan's behavior, which Larry intensified by dictating how mother and son should relate. When Bryan erupted into full-blown crisis, Larry presented Sharon with a choice: Desert her son in favor of marriage or reaffirm her parent-child attachment at the expense of marriage. To opt for marriage would be at immense cost to Bryan and to her own emotional well-being as a mother. To choose Bryan's care would forfeit her marriage.

Parent-child attachments are deeply rooted biological and psychological realities. They are normal mechanisms that ensure survival of the young. Parents will, before all else, act to protect their children and ensure their comfort. This attachment does not automatically move over to make room for a new marriage, even though our cultural psychological wisdom insists that the marital bond take priority to produce a healthy family. This is true for nuclear families in which the couple relationship predates, biologically shares, and has a common genetic interest in the well-being of offspring. It is not true for stepfamilies. In the first few years of stepfamily life, unshared parent-child alliances are in direct competition for priority with spousal alliances. When a zero sum choice must be made between competing loyalties—where one subsystem must win over another—stress escalates dramatically and symptoms erupt.

Stepfamilies are upside-down when compared to nuclear families. When children in nuclear families have problems, it is often because marital conflict puts pressure on children. Children react to disruption between their parents. However, in remarried families, pressure flows *upward* from children to the couple. Stepfamily children lack the deep emotional stake in their parents' new marriage that is typical of nuclear families. On the other hand, remarried parents have an immense stake in what happens to their children. Symptoms in remarried couples are often a result of problems in children. Instead of happy parents creating happy children, happy children in a stepfamily seem to promote happy couples and cohesive stepfamilies.[8] This requires remarried couples to persevere in a marriage with a weak marital-sexual bond in order *first* to care for children and stepchildren. Bonding in remarried couples is secondary to effective stepparenting and parenting.

At the very least, remarried couples bond in a complex, crowded family context. Newlyweds must attend constantly to who is present, who may be listening, and who may be affected by the typical emotional and sexual activities of new couples. Most will have no break from parenting, so it is not a matter of *if* children are included; it is a matter of *how*. This has practical implications for dating relationships and how remarrying couples plan for a new household.

First, it is often easier for couples to date than to pry time out of a shared family calendar. Children can be less resentful about dating parents, and friends are likely to care for children and offer support in hope that a single person's loneliness will end. Couples moving toward remarriage may want to strengthen their attachment by taking more time in courtship before facing the stress of stepfamily life. This also offers a couple time to explore and plan realistically for integrating two single-parent families. Extended courtship, however, has its own tensions of supporting separate households, separating at night, and deferring the desire to be married.

Second, remarrying couples must be realistic about marital expectations and how parent-child attachments will affect their life together. Unrealistic expectations result in painful disillusionment. Consulting with a pastoral counselor or family therapist who has extensive experience working with stepfamilies will help a couple clarify expectations and plan how they will maintain bonding activities in the face of powerful stepfamily forces.

Because children are at the center of the remarriage bonding process, marital attachment is a family task. The couple must somehow recruit

---

[8]Bray and Kelly, *Stepfamilies,* 182.

children and stepchildren into supporting the couple's relationship development process. This requires tender coordination of adult needs, children's needs, and the systemic needs of the emerging stepfamily. If tightly fused parent-child bonds are forced to relax abruptly to make room for a dominant marital dyad, parents and children will both react. Parents will hesitate to negotiate child-free time for couple needs in order to protect their children. They will dread their children's abandonment fears and anxious reactions. Experienced parents know that anxious children do not hesitate to use formidable parent-controlling behavior when their emotional priority with a parent is threatened. At the same time, remarrying people must succeed in gaining time alone to establish their priority as a couple. This early marital balancing act is laced with anxiety and sighs for the relief of redemptive grace. Children's needs cannot be put on hold because their parents have remarried. Neither can they be expected to give up symbolically important attention so it can be given to another person. Yet remarrying parents have adult developmental needs and require time alone to form a secure bond. Children will have to share something they alone had in a single-parent family. Grief recapitulates as parents and children feel the necessary losses.

Successful couples find ways to cooperate with children and stepchildren. Together they manage to set boundaries around the couple strong enough to ensure time and space for bonding tasks, but flexible enough to invite children and their anxiety into the process. However, this requires that new couples learn to communicate and problem solve before marital attachment is secure. Larry and Sharon could not do this. Their attachment was not constant enough to manage the anxiety and stress related to their family's problems. Consequently, intense parent-child attachments and the vicissitudes of early stepfamily tasks derailed their relationship. Both their marriage and their children suffered.

STRESS, ROLE COMPLEXITY, AND TOXIC CONFLICT

That stepfamilies are stressful is no surprise. It is not so obvious that chronic, intense stress is a long-term reality for adults and children who live in stepfamilies. The landmark Developmental Issues in Stepfamilies research project (DIS)[9] found that stress scores for new stepmothers were three times higher than for their first-married counterparts. Remarried men's scores were more than twice as high as first-married husbands. Such high levels of stress interrupt communication and problem solving, and predispose couples to stress-related symptoms. Some social scientists argue that the enduring

---

[9]Bray and Kelly, *Stepfamilies,* 105–6.

costs of stress in stepfamilies may outweigh the benefits of remarriage.[10] Remarrying couples must manage not only our insanely competitive, fast-paced, overworking American culture but also stepfamily-specific challenges: rapid multiple changes, a complex web of ill-defined family relationships, and toxic conflict. All couples can be harmed by the fatigue, depression, anxiety, moodiness, and physical pain that attend chronic stress. Remarrying couples have much more than their share.

Rapid change. Every marriage requires significant adjustment. Couples must negotiate living space and learn to collaborate with another individual in a shared life. For divorced and remarried people, change is usually massive and unpredictable. A cascading pressure of transition starts just before the wedding and reaches peak velocity within a few months. Sharon and Larry, for example, were required to alter their living arrangements, their family rules, and individual roles almost immediately. Though they worked hard to anticipate how they would manage household details, reality only slightly resembled their expectations. Within days of their wedding, rules the couple had negotiated about couple time, boundaries with children, and children's behavior fell victim to the vicissitudes of real life. Neither Larry nor Sharon could tolerate the pressure of their children's reactions to new roles or the dystonic feelings created by new positions in their new family.

As a woman, Sharon faced special struggles in changing her single-parent household. She had worked hard to survive and was secure in ownership of her space, time, position with her children, and money. As a single parent, her sense of identity, strength, and value had blossomed. But this was threatened by her new marriage. Leslie, a single parent for five years, recorded similar feelings in her journal:

> 11-1-99 Monday, All Saints Day.
>
> Less than five days till the wedding and still there are moments, even hours, when I am flooded with feelings of panic, "Can I do this?" I thought I would savor this time, holding every moment close as I replayed scene after scene for my simple pleasure. How can I be so terribly anxious about marrying someone I love passionately, someone who I believe is God's gift to me?
>
> I worry about how everything will fit together—all our things and our bodies and our moods and our preferences—in this small house. I worry about having the cart before the horse—choosing a spouse when I already

---

[10]E. Hetherington and Kathleen Jodl, "Stepfamilies as Settings for Child Development," in *Stepfamilies: Who Benefits? Who Does Not?* ed. Alan Booth and Judy Dunn (Hillsdale, N.J.: Lawrence Erlbaum Associates, 1994).

have children, so that my choice dictates their lives. Is this fair? Not really. They have little to say about it. Although, truly, they could have made my choice nigh to impossible if they'd wanted to prevent it...

Still, Chelsea and I both broke down in our grief over relinquishing what we've had and making room for another who we both fear...will displace the unique intimacy we've shared as an all-female household. It's so hard to give up something you've fought so tenaciously to create and then to preserve. It's the grief of soldiers who, by bonding together through the greatest trauma of their lives, have survived against all odds, and then must disband and leave the very foxhole that protected them. I even feel that way about this old house. This old house has been our foxhole in which we have survived all manner of trauma and abuse, fearing for our lives, fearing we might lose each other forever. Amongst unfaithfulness and betrayal, this house has stood steady and secure, a faithful friend.

Now, we're opening its walls to include another who comes in with new revitalizing ideas. Remodeling plans blanket my dining room table. For as much as my head celebrates this as a good thing, my heart screams, "Wait, you are going too fast. These walls are as sacred as the woods of my youth...These walls have held me like a mother, refusing to let go against all manner of violence. These walls have witnessed my defeat and decomposition, have heard my naked screams and my prayers uttered between the ragged breaths of hyperventilation, and they have never failed to keep me safe. This house is mine, the only thing in my life that has ever been wholly mine. Do not easily ask me to widen my boundaries or tear down its walls. This house is a part of me, a deep cavern of my soul."

No wonder I have felt like our plans were proceeding too quickly. How can I effectively say good-bye to what we've had, so to make room for something new?[11]

Remarrying couples need extra measures of grace, hope, and love to manage the unstable soil characteristic of new stepfamily marriages.

Role Complexity. After years of clinical observation and research, Emily and John Visher[12] concluded that stepfamilies are the most complicated of all family forms. When two single-parent families join, a complex web of relationships coalesces to define the new family. Couples and children are caught squarely in the middle of a sticky, volatile maze that includes pre-existing relationships that are hostile toward the newly formed stepfamily. As a result, couples are faced with chronic relational and emotional overload that drains their energy and hinders important developmental tasks.

---

[11]Thanks to Leslie S. Kendrick, Ph.D., for sharing her journal entries.

[12]Emily Visher and John Visher, *Stepfamilies: A Guide to Working with Stepparents and Stepchildren* (New York: Brunner/Mazel, 1979), 23.

In workshops with remarrying couples, I often use figures 2, 3, and 4 to illustrate changes in relationships and stepfamily complexity. Figure 2 represents Larry Willis' family prior to divorce. It outlines the usual relationships a nuclear family negotiates in daily living. For simplicity, I have restricted this to three generations without aunts, uncles, or other extended family.

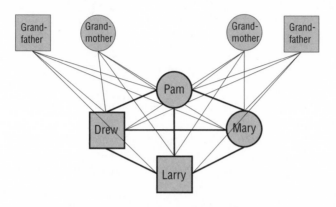

Figure 2
Larry Willis' Nuclear Family

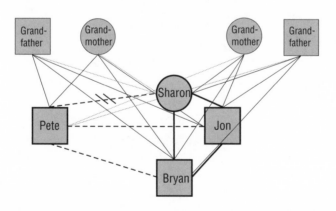

Figure 3
Sharon Brooks's Single-Parent Family

Notice that relationships appear to be relatively clear. It is easy to see how connections between people can be supportive and varied enough to stimulate relational growth.

Figure 3 shows Sharon Brooks' well-established single-parent family that supported her and her children for five years. While nontraditional, relationships are still clear, and roles can be well defined. Now look at figure 4.

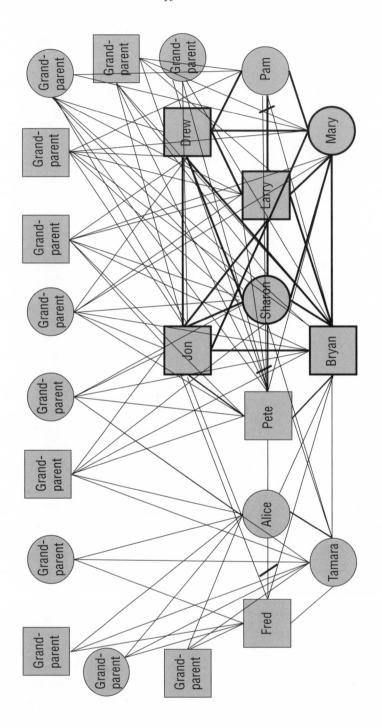

Figure 4
Larry and Sharon Willis' Stepfamily

When confronted with this diagram, remarried couples are frequently startled.[13] Many exclaim, "That takes my breath away!" They then affirm how closely the diagram matches their experience. Instead of feeling embedded in a close emotional structure (as in figs. 2 and 3), these couples are overwhelmed by the intensity of the sheer number of relationships that must be negotiated in a typical stepfamily arrangement. The picture itself feels hopelessly confusing. Who is in? Who is out? Where are the boundaries? Who belongs to whom? What do we call all these people? Who is supposed to do what? When? And, of course, the inevitable, Who is at odds with whom? Who is feeling cheated by lack of attention at the moment? Who is feeling the most pressure to manage all this complexity? When remarried families see their relational environment graphically represented, the weight of relational overload quickly rises to the surface. For the first time many understand why they feel smothered. They live daily in a tangled jungle of relationships that demand constant negotiation. It is hard for those who do not live in stepfamilies to comprehend how confusing this is in daily life.

Relational complexity and role confusion merge in remarried households. Newlyweds who are already parents and ex-spouses are now required to find additional roles as new spouse, instant stepparent, disciplinarian split between various sets of children, new in-law, old outlaw, and who knows what to their partner's ex-spouse, ex-aunts, new uncles, new cousins, and ex-grandparents. Roles become confused, and boundaries are ambiguous. Questions without clear answers arise for newly remarried couples: As a stepparent, do I still fulfill some parental role when the natural ex-spouse parent is present? Who am I when my new wife is discussing financial or custody arrangements with her ex-husband? Do my parental and marital responsibilities change when one set of children is away for visitation? Lacking positive traditions and cultural models for guidance, remarried couples experience significant discomfort in what some researchers have called role strain. This factor may be one of the most significant predictors of marital satisfaction or dissatisfaction in remarried couples[14] High levels of role strain are strongly correlated with low levels of marital satisfaction. Clear roles and unambiguous boundaries seem to provide a context for marital satisfaction and relational growth.

Despite the increasing number of stepfamilies, remarrying couples are mostly left to their own devices to sort through new relationships and manage role strain. New normative roles suggested by popular writers have not

---

[13]Figure 4 includes Pete's new wife and Jon and Bryan's new stepmother.

[14]Doni Whitsett and Helen Land, "Role Strain, Coping, and Marital Satisfaction of Stepparents," *Families in Society: The Journal of Contemporary Human Services* 73, no. 2 (1992):79–92.

been tested by time and are not embedded in our cultural memory. Some people find these innovations helpful. Others are distressed because they cannot make these expert suggestions "work" in the confusion and turmoil of early stepfamily life. The DIS Project[15] provides some of the most helpful information to date. This study, conducted with more than two hundred stepfamilies over fifteen years, shows that remarried couples organize their roles around perceptions of how their marriage *should* work. Three stepfamily forms emerged: (1) neotraditional, which is a reconstruction of a two-parent nuclear family; (2) matriarchal, in which a new male spouse supports a dominant wife/mother who has primary responsibility for all but the couple relationship; and (3) romantic, in which the couple's emotional connection is central and is expected to recreate quickly a harmonious nuclear-like family. Each of these have strengths and weaknesses, though clarity of roles and marital satisfaction tended to be higher in either neotraditional or matriarchal remarriages. These two forms of stepfamily survived more often than romantic remarriages.

Bonding constancy in remarried couples is enhanced by successfully negotiating roles and boundaries in stepfamily life. These undergird a couple struggling with communication and problem solving in complex stepfamily living. It seems to make little difference what roles are or where boundaries are drawn, so long as the couple agrees. On the other hand, romantic remarriage relies on an imitation of nuclear family processes that centralize couple bonding. Roles and boundaries are subservient to a romantic vision and are rarely reliable enough to support a new stepfamily. These newly remarried couples collapse quickly under stress.

Research is just beginning to explore how successful remarried couples manage relational complexity. We know very little about what roles and boundaries are effective in stepfamily life. In addition, our culture has not come to terms with stepfamilies. It offers no consistent tradition for appropriate positive stepfamily living. Couples pay the price with interrupted bonding and stunted relationship development.

Toxic conflict. In their book *It Takes Two*, Andy and Judy Lester suggest that intimate relationships cannot exist without conflict, and love cannot escape anger. Couples who avoid anger fail to develop deep levels of intimacy. Conflict in marriage, they rightly claim, can be a vehicle of growth "rather than the hammer which destroys a marriage…Blessed is the spouse whose partner is committed to dealing openly and honestly with angry feelings."[16] Though these authors are concerned primarily with first-married couples,

---

[15]Bray and Kelly, *Stepfamilies*.

[16]Andy Lester and Judy Lester, *It Takes Two* (Louisville: Westminster John Knox Press, 1998), 88–89.

their observations are true also for remarried couples. Successful couples are honest about feelings and actively seek to resolve anger.

However, remarried couples have trouble with conflict management. Most live in a relationally crowded environment. There is as little privacy for arguing as there is for sexual expression. Emotionally precocious children are listening, and their history of divorce has sensitized them to adult moods. They will be sharply attuned to their own vulnerability to embattled adults' decisions. When their newly remarried parents argue, children react to an internal call: Choose sides because disaster is coming! Children are reactive to marital conflict and quickly jump to their parent's rescue. Likewise, hypervigilant parents will passionately protect their vulnerable children's feelings. This dynamic, along with recapitulated grief activated by conflict, overwhelming stress of new stepfamily life, and role confusion, adds an emotional load to conflict that is unique to stepfamilies. Conflict shifts smoothly from growth-producing opportunity to toxic contamination of the bonding process.

Children-in-the-middle conflict, a hallmark of stepfamily living, is exquisitely painful and a robust toxin. It is present in most remarried couples' arguments.

Jan and Steve sought counseling after their first year of marriage to help with financial problems. Initially, they presented a simple picture—Steve worked full-time, and Jan worked part-time, yet there was never enough money to pay their bills. They rarely bought extras or paid for entertainment. Jan blamed the problem on Steve's lack of motivation. He had turned down several management jobs because he did not want the stress. Steve blamed Jan because she refused to find full-time employment and did not manage money efficiently.

By the end of the first session, their conflict became clear. Children were firmly wedged in the emotional core of their distress. Steve resented money Jan spent on her twelve-year-old daughter Vicki's expensive after-school treats and the food she wasted as a "finicky" eater. He was also tired of paying for her weekend movies, costly piano lessons, and gymnastics. He felt he was bearing too many of his stepdaughter's expenses while Jan kept a low-paying job with flexible hours. Steve knew Jan wanted to be home for Vicki in the afternoons and to participate in her school activities, but he felt he was being used. Jan countered his thrust with her parry—the couple had agreed to this prior to marriage. "Aha!" exclaimed Steve, "That was while Vicki's father was still paying child support." They had planned for this income to continue, but it had ended shortly after the wedding. Jan had refused to pursue her ex-husband for failed child support. She feared retaliation and intrusion from her ex-spouse. Steve believed she was protecting Vicki's father and taking advantage of his own generous nature. To make matters worse, Jan resisted any money that he wanted to spend on his own children beyond his court-ordered support. Why could she indulge Vicki and he not give his children a few extras? They had no piano lessons, no parent at their school, and had to come home alone. Was that fair?

In tears, Jan spoke about feeling "punished for being a good mother." She also felt guilty about standing firm for what she believed was right. She had worked hard to negotiate these important issues prior to marriage, but at the same time she was forced to depend on Steve's generosity when Vicki's father failed her. She was trapped. She couldn't help resenting Steve for sending so much to his children when their own finances were failing, and she saw Vicki suffering because she got nothing from her father. When conflict erupted, her guilt pushed her to blame Steve for keeping a job he liked rather than opting for more money. Simple money management issues had become toxic for Jan and Steve. Anxious emotional attachment to their children clouded their judgment and kept them reactive to each other.

Jan and Steve were able to sort through the emotional maze that guided their anger and to learn skills to negotiate some resolution. They learned to respect each other's tenderness for their own children and found ways to approach each other about scary, potentially toxic child and ex-spouse issues. Together they looked at Jan's child support problems. By reading about stepfamilies, they learned that pursuing lost support from a hostile ex-spouse often means added legal expense, more conflict with children in the middle, and increased interference. Together they weighed their options and decided they were at a critical point in their marriage and stepfamily. Now was not the best time to risk conflict with an ex-spouse. They decided not to pursue child support until their new family could tolerate the risks. Instead, they would review their budget and decide together what to adjust so earlier agreements could be honored. It would be hard, but they would try. They also agreed that in the future, either of them could ask for a therapist-consultant when they felt a problem was too frightening or toxic to sort out alone.

Toxic conflict was lurking just under the surface of Jan and Steve's marriage. Once it was exposed, they were able to talk about it and manage problem solving. Their attachment was supported, and they left counseling feeling hopeful about their marriage.

Remarried couples fight about household chores, outside activities, recreation, affection, and sex like any other marital pair. However, remarried couples are likely to argue less about these and more about child-related issues.[17] Mundane disagreement spins quickly out of control when it touches children. As Steve and Jan illustrate, financial issues almost always carry questions of who is supporting whom. Since more than half of divorced fathers do not pay their ordered support, financial conflict carries extra emotional weight for many remarried couples.

When children are the center of a newly remarried couple's conflict, the potential for toxic contamination of normal marital conflict escalates rapidly. In the early years of remarriage, anger and disagreement can ignite a marital meltdown able to lay waste to the entire stepfamily system. Couple attachment stalls; relationship development ends; and, as with Larry and Sharon, a new marriage falls to earth in a fiery crash of "irreconcilable differences" and tumbles into the morass of another divorce.

Unlike Steve and Jan, Larry and Sharon faced the iridescent glow of reactive child-centered conflict from the first day of their marriage. They considered living arrangements at length but missed other important steps. First, they failed to consider how they would integrate new stepparents into their children's lives and how fast that should happen. They also failed to discuss what kind of stepparent-stepchild relationships they would encourage and what kind their children were likely to tolerate. Children were not consulted. As an enthusiastic parent, Larry expected Sharon's sons to welcome his structure and masculine role model. He assumed the boys would want intimacy, which they never had with their biological father. Larry, however, missed the fact that Bryan and Jon did not want another parent. They resisted his initiative and became reactive, and Larry was hurt. Sharon, concerned for her children's welfare, could not respond when Larry turned to her for support and soothing. Larry became discouraged and emotionally backed away from Sharon and her sons. On one occasion, Sharon exploded and told Larry he was just like her "ex," whom she did not respect and deeply disliked. This set the stage for couple alienation and fiery reactivity between Larry, Bryan, and Sharon.

Sharon made several mistakes of her own. Without thoughtful negotiation of her role, she assumed Larry's children would treat her like a wicked stepmother and kept her distance from them. She did not expect them to love her but did expect some respect as "the mother of the house." She hoped that out of this, friendship might grow. However, Larry's children refused to eat food she cooked and did not show appreciation for her

---

[17]Research suggests that first-married couples will argue about household chores, sex, and in-laws. Remarried couples are much more likely to argue about children and proper conduct than any other single element of their marriage. Charles Hobart, "Conflict in Remarriages," *Journal of Divorce and Remarriage* 15, no. 3 (1991): 69–86; Whitsett and Land, *Role Strain*.

household work. This proved to her she had become the wicked stepmother. In frustration Sharon sought support from Larry, which did not materialize. Instead of empathizing with her pain, Larry sided with his children by telling her she was "cold" and should try harder to attach as "a mom." Toxic couple conflict quickly followed his suggestion that she might "win the kids over with honey instead of vinegar." Covertly supported by their parents, the children resisted ambiguous stepparent roles. Parents colluded with their children and became reactive to each other and to opposing sets of "enemy" offspring. Communication and problem solving failed, and couple bonding was interrupted. Disaster was not far behind.

SOCIAL SUPPORT

Healthy couples need good systems of social support. Remarried couples, however, seldom receive the same level of support from families, friends, or extended social networks as the first-married.[18] This stands in tension with the fact they are more likely to need places for safe retreat from complex circumstances. Newly remarried couples often cannot manage the full weight of stepfamily pain *in* the marriage. They need relationships outside the marriage with nonreactive, caring persons who will help them support their commitments. Friends and close family members can provide a safe haven, a "reality check," and an empathic ear to hear the pain of struggle. First-married couples count on time away from friends and family; remarried couples need the affirmation, support, and sometimes assistance from trusted people who remain close by and help them balance communication and problem solving while attachment constancy is developing.

In *When Religion Gets Sick*, Wayne Oates[19] describes how resources found in healthy religion promote health. He contends that people are kept "sound" by supportive guidance through life passages by a healthy and hope-giving community. One of the church's primary tasks is to help people in transition find their new place in the religious community and then define its relationship to them. When this breaks down, spiritual nourishment cuts off and vulnerable people become isolated, spiritually undernourished, and "sick." Resources and rites of passage that could help newly remarried couples endure or thrive are withheld. Hurting couples are left alone, and stepfamilies fail.

---

[18]See, for instance, Lawrence Kurdek, "Social Support and Psychological Distress in First-married and Remarried Newlywed Husbands and Wives," *Journal of Marriage and the Family* 51 (1989):1047–52; Marilyn Ihinger-Tallman and Kay Pasley, "Remarriage and Integration Within the Community," *Journal of Marriage and the Family* 48 (1986): 395–405; William Walsh, "Twenty Major Issues in Remarriage Families," *Journal of Counseling and Development* 70 (1992):709–15.

[19]Wayne Oates, *When Religion Gets Sick* (Philadelphia: Westminster Press, 1970), 81–100.

Many remarried couples feel abandoned. This is usually unintentional. Congregations are uncertain about how to respond without clear roles, boundaries, and rituals for welcoming newly remarried couples. How much space does a newly remarried couple need? How much initiative should be taken to invite the new couple and their family to social events? Is their resistance to invitation a form of rejection, or are other factors, such as time pressure or social fear, at work in the new couple? Newly remarried couples can easily put off family, friends, and congregational carers while sorting through confusion and complexity. In circumstances that feel overwhelming, most have little energy to pursue any further demand. Pastoral carers who wish to encourage remarriage development must be careful to maintain a supportive presence without adding pressure.

Where Rivers Meet

Stepfamilies live and die by how remarried couples fare. Family cohesion, the sense of "we-ness" that sustains a common life, relies on a marital dyad that bonds and grows toward mutuality. The clean, clear epigenetic relationship cycle in which stages successively build on a foundation set in bonding may reflect "normal" first-married couple development. However, remarried couples face a trying conundrum. Experience, supported by research, shows that a strong marital bond is the key developmental task for all stepfamilies, just as it is in nuclear families. It provides a platform for the family and supports the couple tasks necessary to survive early stepfamily life. Yet bonding and marital satisfaction do not come first for remarried couples. Instead, they seem to be *outcomes* of surviving the turmoil of early remarried life and producing a context that includes happy children. Pastoral care that relies on images of first marriage will miss this core dilemma for remarried couples.

Success for remarried couples is complex. Life begins when several streams meet and contribute diverse colors, personalities, sediments, and temperatures to flow in a new direction. Emotional ghosts from the past intermingle with the joy of newfound love. Couple bonding merges with parental responsibilities and deep attachments to children. Leftover legal and financial burdens boil into the flow, bringing muddy silt from nearby swamps. Together this mix tumbles over a ledge and downhill through the rocky bed of stepfamily life. Many things happen at once. Somehow, couple attachment and its developmental cycle must collapse into a dense, tightly packed, accelerating force that can survive multiple collisions, jumbled purposes, and the pressure of intense stress. A couple must maintain enough separateness, control, and composure to look both upstream and down, across temporal boundaries. Looking backward means claiming the purpose and desire that sustained dating and risk-taking in remarriage. Looking ahead means watching for safe eddies in common parenting, anticipating dangerous problems with children, and hoping for quieter water with less stress and more time for couple development. This is not easy. Most will simply scramble to survive.

During the difficult early years of remarriage, successful couples must do three things: They must nurture their adult relationship; they must develop a mutual vision of marriage and stepfamily life; and they *must* learn to cooperate and support each other in parenting and child-related issues. This last task is the single most important factor in remarried couple development. It guides the couple through critical issues of early stepfamily life— parenting children and integrating a stepparent (especially stepfathers) into children's lives—and provides an anchor for couple attachment through the breathtaking changes and toxic conflict inherent in early remarriage.

Remarried Couples and their Stories: A Pastoral Perspective

Remarried couple's stories are woven from a different fabric than the first-married. In chapter three, we explored how meaning is derived through structuring experience into stories. Stories create the substance of lives and relationships. Philosopher Michel Foucault refines this by suggesting that we ascribe meaning to our experience through a stock of culturally available discourses that are generally accepted as appropriate and representative of certain aspects of life. First marriage in a nuclear family provides the pattern for discourse about marriage in our culture. We do not know how to talk about, or symbolize, effective marriage in any other way. It is our institutionally established vision. It organizes, registers, and classifies how couples are to be together and how they are to behave. Stories of first-married success and failure tell researchers, clinicians, marriage experts, pastors, and the public what to expect and how to judge a marriage as good or bad.

This cultural narrative is powerful and unconsciously accepted. Remarried couples use it to discount their own experience and their own knowledge about their marriages. Through it, they are incited to bend their stories to fit cultural expectations and so lose integrity with their own experience. Their own story is hidden and subjugated; the stories they live out by default to the dominant narrative are problem saturated and deformed. Without validation or voice, remarried couples' stories are exiled from the legitimate domain of established truth.[20]

---

[20]See particularly the thought of Michel Foucault in: *Power/Knowledge: Selected Interviews and Other Writings* (New York: Pantheon Books, 1980) and *The Archaeology of Knowledge* (New York: Pantheon Books, 1972).

Remarried couples do not fit easily into normative schemas such as epigenetic couple development with discrete cycles, established wedding rituals, models of marital conflict management, or even the usual expected context of time alone for newlyweds. Larry and Sharon are good examples of how easily a remarrying couple are overwhelmed by a cultural "truth" of "the good marriage." When they could find no valid categories to contain their own embodied experience, their story quickly became problem saturated. There was no shared language to voice their story, so it was forced into a mold that could not hold it. Pastoral carers often meet couples at this crucial intersection. Life fails to make sense when lived experience finds no connection with acceptable truth. Confusion reigns, and couples stagger beneath a load of unrealized expectation with no support from a guiding narrative. Vitality is extinguished, and couples die. Pastoral care must act to enliven the spirits of remarrying couples. They must be empowered to find voice for their own unique subjugated stories. Once voiced, the community of care must join with couples to help construct a new communal narrative that includes the lived reality of emergent remarried stories.

To borrow and expand Foucault's thought, remarried couples are twice exiled. First, they are exiled from the symbols, rituals, formal discourse, and accepted knowledge about marriage contained by the central cultural narrative. Their "indigenous" knowledge is pushed to the periphery of community life in favor of validating, supporting, and securing the value of first marriage. Second, because of this marginalization, they are also exiled from their own experience. It does not match the dominant narrative and is therefore invalid. With no language to articulate their subjugated, lower-order marital knowledge, discourse is impossible. Remarried couples are left with an internalized, normalizing judgment that their unions are inadequate. Their choice: Deny and distort their experience until it can be folded discretely into the dominant narrative or remain marginal and invalid. In either case, remarried couples' stories will be problem saturated and tentative.

PASTORAL CARE AND EXILES

> By the waters of Babylon,
> > there we sat down and wept,
> > when we remembered Zion.
> On the willows there
> > we hung up our lyres,
> For there our captors
> required of us songs,
> and our tormentors, mirth, saying,
> > "Sing us one of the songs of Zion."
> > > (Psalm 137:1–3, RSV)

Bereft of a place in community and separated from their own experience, remarried couples begin life in psychological homelessness and exile. Alone and still grieving past losses, they face an unpredictable, chaotic wilderness with few instructions for survival and only vague impressions of the way to a longed-for "home." Biblical tradition is no stranger to exile. It is at the heart of Hebrew Scripture and the gospel of Christ. It is a metaphor introducing us to a God who redeems people from the margins of life, gives them a new story grounded in their own subjugated experience, and then provides them with a home replete with new rituals and symbols.

Exile to Babylon was an extraordinary formative factor for Judeo-Christian self-understanding. It is a story of broken promises, violated covenants, and the destruction of faith-sustaining symbols. No longer could the nation look to the temple and its rituals, the Davidic kingdom and its promise, or a homeland that could nurture and generate a future. These were destroyed and could never again be recreated in exactly the same form. Disorganized, uprooted, and beaten, the exiles found themselves by the waters of Babylon with no language to describe their alienation from their own history, their relationship to God, or how they would relate to their new reality. By the waters of Babylon, they faced identity-destroying absorption into the dominant culture or marginalization. In the crucible of loss and despair, they confronted two profound questions: Without the symbols and rituals that sustained our ancestors and formerly gave us meaning, who, now, are we? Can God still be with us? Prophetic honesty about sin, loss, and responsibility loosened subjugated stories and a new community with a refined self-understanding emerged out of the wreckage of the old. Israel resumed life as a people. Discourse of loss and recovery molded a prophetic theology of exile, restoration, and new covenant. It paved the way for a new vision of God's action on behalf of the fallen and set the stage for the subversive gospel of Christ.

The prophets' message proclaimed God's ongoing grace in Israel's captivity, even when circumstances demanded judgment and destruction. Chained to the exiles' deep groan of lament for sin and failure is a corresponding cry for God's love, presence, and mercy. It is a cry of lost connection and homelessness that finds its fulfillment only in utter dependence on God's faithfulness and willingness to restore. This divine restorative nature is so imbedded in creation that it is organically present in the depth of loss and lament itself. At the heart of pain is the cry of separation and longing—"*Oh, God!*" It contains primal and unconscious knowledge that God's renewing spirit is present in the depths of despair.

…[T]hey were rebellious in their purposes,
    and were brought low through their iniquity.
Nevertheless he regarded their distress,
    when he heard their cry.
He remembered for their sake his covenant,
and relented according to the abundance of his steadfast love…
Save us, O LORD, our God,
    and gather us from among the nations,
that we may give thanks to thy holy name
and glory in thy praise.

                    (Psalm 106:43–45, 47, RSV)

God's restoration is not found by pretending to be a never-fallen participant in symbols lost to sin, but in utter reliance on God's continued connection to us in our failure. Exiles are empowered by God's faithfulness to lay hands to their own release and join with God in the overwhelming task of building new homes in a desolate wasteland. "Who, now, are we?" thereby finds its answer in the story of exile and restoration itself. "We are those who have fallen and whom God has saved." Smoldering wreckage is converted to an orienting symbol, and recovery is described by new covenants and transformed ritual. Together, these sustain captives who return home to reorganize the rubble of their past. The exile's story becomes a texture of hope and an expression of promise. This is possible because prophetic vision helps name the truth of captives' experience and locates God's activity in loss and lament. Prophetic care calls exiles to integrity with their story and points to a vocation that defies cultural narratives that rob them of promise and discourage their faith. In this the nature of God is revealed.

Like exiled Israel, divorced and remarrying couples have survived the destruction of their sustaining symbols, meanings, and rituals. They long for a restored homeland that can never be reclaimed in its original form. Out of the depths of loss arise questions of an exile, "Now that our homeland and all it represents has been lost, who, now, are we?" or, more clearly, "In the face of failure and broken covenants, what, now, is marriage?" Like the prophets of exile and restoration, pastoral carers must help divorced and remarried people find voice for their lament and an interpretation of their story in the light of God's promise. If there is hope, it arises from the ashes of divorce. If there is sustaining symbol, it is arranged and created from the fragments of loss and broken promises. If there is recovery, it is voiced in the language of hope for remarriage and ritualized in honest-to-experience covenants. If there is a song to be sung, it will be loss in counterpoint with hope and the grace of reconstruction in tension with the judgment of exile.

PROPHETIC PASTORAL CARE

Prophetic pastoral care for exiles is not expert advice. It is care that empowers stories, gives voice to truth, asks hard questions that have no answer, and envisions a redemptive future. By articulating this vision, the church calls remarrying people to a restorative vocation. Prophetic care is also subversive as it empowers remarried couples to defy cultural narratives that undermine their unique strengths, quench their hope, and relegate them to a marginalized, substandard existence. The mission of the church, expressed through prophetic pastoral care, is to voice God's promised restoration and act to empower couples and congregations to live into God's redeeming activity.

Prophetic care weeps with the exiles' lament. It holds tight to remorse for sin and then responds to assure of God's forgiveness. It shares the sorrow of tragic loss and the rage of recognized injustice. Only then can it articulate God's loving compassion and promise of restoration. Empowering care helps remarried couples identify experience, name reality, and story their embodied truth with integrity. Guided by such care, remarrying people can interpret their new covenant with God and with each other. They are empowered to begin reconstructing symbols that defy the subjugating challenge of the dominant cultural narrative.

From this foundation in prophecy and subversive empowerment, important questions find practical relevance. For example: What is *re*marriage? If a neat, clean, nuclear developmental process is impossible, what truths can the lives of remarried people tell us about how attachment takes place in a stepfamily? If established marriage liturgies and ceremonies that enliven first-married couples fail to symbolize remarried reality, what does this mean for the church and remarrying couples? Must remarrying people enforce their own second-class status by forcing themselves into a covenant meant for someone else? Must they promise what cannot be delivered because their past includes children and a living ex-spouse to whom they also made promises? What do ceremonies and liturgies offer to remarrying people who have lost faith in promise itself? What are remarrying people really promising to each other, the community, and God? What does the community of faith promise them? Who are their children to them?

Asked in the positive, prophetic pastoral care wonders: What might listening to the rarely talked about experience of marginalized remarried couples tell us about new, or enlivening, symbols for a remarriage commitment? How might the community of faith help couples articulate their promises and provide support and accountability? How can unique remarriage promises be symbolized and connected to the restoring work of the community of faith? If there is no cultural guide for remarried success, what can we learn from the unique outcomes of successful remarried couples? How is this integrated into our Christian story and the church's culturally subversive ministry? Finally, how does a remarried couple's commitment to a vocation of reconstruction instruct the church?

Prophetic pastoral care claims no clear answer or expert advice. It engages the exile's story and asks questions that challenge couples and the community of faith to transforming action. It names sin and tragedy and knows that *re*marriage is not the same as *marriage*. There are too many generations involved and too many people complicating the scene. Circumstances have changed, and the homeland is polluted by ash and rubble. Remarriage, after all, begins in broken promise and loss of faith in covenant. Prophetic care knows that a new covenant cannot be the old one said harder. Instead it must symbolize the remarrying exile's history of loss, captivity, and God's restoration. In listening love, care raises the prophet's measuring line of God's restoring grace (Zech. 1:14–17).

Listening love and prophetic discourse will not miss the fact that a new song is not soon separated from the fatigue of a long wilderness walk or the humiliation of sifting through ashes for building materials. A home may well result, but at high cost. For returning Babylonian refugees, there is no parting Red Sea, no water in the desert, no miracle of quail, and no seven-day march around Jericho with triumphant ram's horn accompaniment. Instead, rubble awaits. Enemies stand by and mock. Bystanders wag their heads in consternation at such folly. The path to reconstruction for remarried couples is a wilderness journey of daily challenges, small successes, and repeated setbacks. Prophetic pastoral care helps couples interpret grace in the many hard days "of small things" (Zech. 4:10) when stepfamily pressure threatens to overcome hope.

As for the postexilic prophets, hope for remarried couples rests in a vision that is both realistic and idealistic. As the prophet proclaims: Times are hard; there is little payoff soon. But let your hands be strong, those of you who have laid your hand to the work of God's restoration. There will be a sowing of peace, and the vine will bear fruit. The ground shall give its increase, and the heavens will produce rain. I, says the Lord of hosts, will cause the remnant of this people to possess all these things. Fear not, but let your hands be strong (based on Zech. 8: 9–13).

In God's economy, exile promises restoration. New symbols, stories, and covenants grow from God's gracious vision. Possibility is lodged in the heart of despair, and promise is embodied in God's presence at the center of the remarried community's life. In this, the glory of God is revealed:

> When the LORD restored the fortunes of Zion,
>> we were like those who dream.
> Then our mouth was filled with laughter,
>> and our tongue with shouts of joy;
> then it was said among the nations,
>> "The LORD has done great things for them."
> The LORD has done great things for us,
>> and we rejoiced.
> Restore our fortunes, O LORD,
>> like the watercourses in the Negeb.
> May those who sow in tears
>> reap with shouts of joy.
> Those who go out weeping,
>> bearing the seed for sowing,
> shall come home with shouts of joy,
>> carrying their sheaves.
>
> (Psalm 126)

In the parable of remarriage, successful couples teach us about God's restoration. They symbolize a new covenant and reveal to the body of Christ how God creates a new thing.

Chapter 6
Interlude: About What We Know

There are three kinds of lies:
Lies, damn lies, and statistics.

Benjamin Disraeli

Last week I drove through Atlanta. I was stuck in traffic and had my radio tuned to the Dr. Laura show. Even though I had never listened to her show before, I knew she was outspoken and known for saying things people didn't want to hear. Her second caller was a man thinking of remarriage. He wanted her opinion about starting his life over again after a divorce. She asked him one question, "Do you have kids?" When he answered yes, she took off. I can't remember her exact words, but I do remember their substance and how much they hurt. No, she said, you don't have a right to remarry. You've already hurt your children enough by divorcing. Why complicate their lives more and make matters worse by putting them in the worst possible environment? She went on to say that research was absolutely clear. Children who live in stepfamilies are pretty well doomed. She talked about a book (I think it was called *The Divorce Culture*) that had all the research proving that children in stepfamilies have almost no chance for a successful life. She said she agreed with the author who talked about how selfish adults were who remarried at the expense of their kids. She finished her "conversation" with this man on the radio by telling him that he was selfish even to think of remarrying. Research proved it could only damage his kids further. All the evidence was against stepfamilies. "Grow up," she said, "and take care of your responsibilities. Stop whining about wanting a second chance for a good relationship. You gave that up when you divorced."

I was stunned. I've lived in a stepfamily for over ten years. My kids, and by that I mean my own and my stepkids, are in college now and doing all right. Even after all this time I felt like I had been slapped in the face and blamed. I turned off the radio and cried for the next hundred miles, replaying every trial my kids had, every failure they endured, every class they failed, and every tear they shed. I felt so caught between humiliation, guilt, and anger. How dare she! How dare she tell me that the family I have come to love so dearly should never have been! How dare she tell me that my children would be better off without the stepparent who helped raise them, who loved them, who supported them! In those minutes listening to her through tears of pain and rage, I decided it was all worth it. Every tear I shed as a parent and stepparent; every problem we had in our marriage because of kids; every sleepless night I had trying to figure out how to be a good parent in this terribly confusing family; it was all worth it. I wouldn't trade my family, my kids, or my stepkids for anything in the world. I would never go back.[1]

Knowledge, Truth, and Politics

As scholars, practitioners, consumers, and concerned parents, Americans love research. We turn to the scientific method to tell us the truth. We rely on polls, averages, and statistical analysis to keep information honest and guarantee certainty about things that are important to us. Our positivist culture tells us that "true" knowledge is based in sound research. We believe that people, beliefs, relationships, and feelings can be objectified, discretely observed, sorted out, and then described through a lens of scientific neutrality. With enough control over classification and methods of observation, we expect researchers to gain special truth that can be transformed into general laws that will explain causes and predict outcomes.

"Doing the research" organizes our thinking, stratifies our economy, and produces normative truths that shape our lives. Nowhere is this more evident than in the study of children of divorced families. As divorce rates peaked, research exploded. We have many questions about how children of divorce fare academically, emotionally, physically, cognitively, and socially. Hundreds of studies using a variety of methods have produced an immense pool of data and a few certain conclusions. This data can be manipulated to prove, at one extreme, that there is no significant difference between children raised in stepfamilies and those from nuclear family homes. At the other extreme, it can show that the difference is so great that stepfamily children are imperiled. What is the truth? What do we really know about children of divorce, especially those in stepfamilies?

---

[1]Unnamed traveler, September, 1999.

Stepfamily studies have provided a few raw pieces of an intricate jigsaw puzzle. We are missing more pieces than we have. But research methods allow us to take partial information and speculate about the complete picture. It is important to understand that research has clear limitations. We must pay careful attention to how it is used, especially in relationship to something as crucial as stepfamilies and their children.

INTERNAL LIMITATIONS

Most stepfamily studies are completed by students and professors in academic settings or are funded for specific public policy concerns. Ethical researchers will use the best methods available and will document procedures so that studies can be replicated to verify their findings. Good researchers know their results are limited and are careful about how they interpret data into conclusions. Research methods themselves are capable only of providing fragments of information that must then be understood through a lens of theory. Few serious scholars expect to find a broad, coherent picture of any population using current methods. As we look at stepfamily research, we must be careful to remember several important factors.

First, almost all research about stepfamilies investigates a clear, carefully defined question with a small, carefully chosen group of people. A hypothesis about some aspect of stepfamily life is constructed, and a procedure is implemented to test it. Most studies use a test population of one hundred people or less to accept or reject a hypothesis. One exception is sociological and demographic research, which uses census or large-poll data to produce general information about population movements or general characteristics of a population. In either case, a legitimate question arises about limitations. Can findings from a small research project, or even several small projects, accurately be generalized to a broader population of stepfamilies? Can inferences from large-poll questions be interpreted accurately to apply to stepfamilies in general? These are complex questions that challenge our most effective researchers and methods.

A second limitation for research is the nature of statistical analysis. Procedures are used to evaluate data to determine whether there is evidence that a hypothesis can be accepted or rejected with some degree of significance. This can be misleading for those unfamiliar with the language of statistics. For instance, a researcher may state that he or she has demonstrated a "significant" difference between nuclear family children and stepfamily children on a test that measures self-esteem. Apart from the fact that this observed difference relies on the validity and reliability of self-esteem tests for a particular population, a finding of "significant difference" means only that a mathematical procedure was applied to two groups of scores, and, according to either an ideal model or statistical norm, the

difference between the two scores was unlikely to have occurred by accident or random chance. "Significance" has nothing to say about how large
the effect actually is or whether it has any significance to a child's life or
future prospects. It means only that there is, for instance, a 95 percent
chance that the difference between the two groups of scores actually exists.
The concept reassures researchers that it is unlikely that all of the difference
they notice in their data is due to measurement error or random chance.

In fact, many significant findings are very small. Furthermore, we can
rarely determine whether an observed difference actually has any clinical,
academic, social, or spiritual significance in any area of life. Most often,
researchers infer what a significant finding may mean to the population
being studied. Such interpretations can range from careful consideration of
possibilities to wild and grand speculation. In either case, studies that show
"significant differences" between divorced family and nuclear family children cannot tell us how children are actually affected or predict which child
is likely to fail in school, act out, or become depressed as a result of surviving divorce or remarriage.

Third, isolating variables for study is difficult in most social science
research and nearly impossible in divorce studies. For example, most
stepfamily authorities feel safe documenting research that shows that children
of divorce have more emotional and behavioral problems, consult
psychologists more often, have more health problems, have more problems
with academic performance, and are more likely to drop out and leave
home earlier than children who live in nuclear families.[2] However, these
almost self-evident facts are not quite so clear. It is easy to use divorced and
non-divorced parents as a single controlling variable. Studies do show several
significant differences when children from divorced and nuclear families
are compared. The problem lies with other complicating factors, such as
chronic parental conflict, which are difficult, if not impossible, to isolate
and measure.

There is evidence that the actual event of divorce or remarriage may
have little to do with childhood problems observed in divorced and remarried families. Some studies suggest that children fare better in single-parent
families and stepfamilies than they do in conflict-ridden nuclear homes.[3]

---

[2]David Popenoe, "The Evolution of Marriage and the Problem of Stepfamilies: A Biosocial Perspective," in *Stepfamilies: Who Benefits? Who Does Not?* ed. Alan Booth and Judy Dunn (Hillsdale, N.J.:
Laurence Erlbaum Associates, 1994).

[3]Florence Kaslow and L. Schwartz, *Dynamics of Divorce: A Life Cycle Perspective* (New York:
Brunner/Mazel, 1987), 6–7; E. Hetherington, M. Cox, and R. Cox, "Effects of Divorce on Parents and
Children," in *Nontraditional Families*, ed. M. Lamb (Hillsdale, N.J.: Lawrence Erlbaum Associates,
1982); N. Long and R. Forehand, "The Effects of Parental Divorce and Marital Conflict on Children:
An Overview," *Journal of Developmental and Behavioral Pediatrics* 8 (1987): 292–96; A. Stolberg et al.,
"Individual, Familial and Environmental Determinants of Children's Post-Divorce Adjustment and
Maladjustment," *Journal of Divorce* 11 (1987): 51–70.

The problem for research is that conflict between biological parents occurs in *both* nuclear families and divorced families. Observing this conflict is complicated. It is ritualized in divorced families and often overlooked when families are "intact." Significant conflict may also take different forms in nuclear and divorced families. How are these complex variables sorted? How is conflict observed and measured in nuclear homes as opposed to divorced families? Do children in nuclear families whose parents stay together in spite of chronic, intense conflict suffer the same difficulties as children of divorce? We do not know. Our knowledge is further limited because few divorce studies account for the positive impact divorce may have on children who experience relief and greater safety when a violent, turbulent, or highly dysfunctional parental union dissolves. It is likely that these factors are "underestimated and underdescribed."[4] Research cannot yet answer these questions. It is important to know that research is limited. It cannot define human behavior precisely or isolate complex variables well enough to guarantee certainty about any observation.

Researchers often find what they expect. This fourth limitation is called research bias and takes many forms. It can be manifested in the way questions are asked, how measurement is constructed, how observation takes place, and how results are interpreted. In one classic example, researchers observed and measured the performance of albino rats that were falsely labeled "maze-bright" and "maze-dull." Predictably, observations verified that "maze-bright" rats performed consistently better in learning a simple maze. This study illustrates that no matter how simple the research design or clear the methodology, when observers expect to find certain results, they generally will.[5] This phenomenon can be complicated by a "positive test strategy." This refers to a principle taught in basic research classes that studies should be constructed within conditions that have a good chance of supporting the research hypothesis.[6] Such strategies raise the probability that a study will be influenced by a researcher's bias or outcome expectations. Bias in research has immense implications for stepfamilies and others who experience prejudice or bias from public policies and popular attitudes.

Finally, much of what we know about children of divorce emerges from clinics where they are treated for problems. This raises several important questions. Are families who seek help actually less functional than those who do not? Do we get a biased picture of stepfamilies by studying problem

---

[4]Kaslow and Schwartz, *Dynamics of Divorce.*

[5]R. Rosenthal, *Experimenter Effects in Behavioral Research* (New York: Irvington, 1976); R. Rosenthal and K. Fode, "The Effect of Experimenter Bias on the Performance of the Albino Rat," *Behavioral Science* 8 (1963): 183–89.

[6]Meredith D. Gall, Walter Borg, and Joyce Gall, *Educational Research, An Introduction,* 6th ed. (White Plains, N.Y.: Longman Publishing, 1996), 481; J. Klayman and Y.-W. Ha, "Confirmation, Disconfirmation, and Information in Hypothesis Testing," *Psychological Review* 94 (1987): 211–28.

families in treatment? Whether this is true or not, can findings from a population of troubled families be generalized to families who do not report problems to therapists? Or conversely, since stepfamilies see therapists more often than nuclear families, does this mean they are more troubled than nuclear families or simply more willing to seek help? Without answers to these and other related questions, findings from clinical research is extremely limited. These studies may help describe clinical methods helpful for stepfamilies, but they hold little value for describing or defining the experience of those who are not in treatment.

A good illustration of research limits is the Developmental Issues in StepFamilies Research Project (DIS),[7] which was funded by the National Institute of Child Health and Human Development. This carefully controlled study was a large longitudinal project that compared 100 stepfamilies with 100 nuclear families over a fifteen-year period. It was guided by experienced researchers and is one of the best stepfamily studies to date. It was also limited by factors inherent in research design. Appropriate subjects had to be selected. Because ethical human research must always be voluntary, subjects were recruited from schools, parent groups, and athletic teams and through referrals from local clergy and media advertisements in the Houston, Texas, metropolitan area. Those who volunteered all had some stake in the project and its outcome. This means that participants were already invested in attitudes and beliefs about stepfamilies or nuclear families before the project began. Furthermore, people who volunteer for research projects share certain characteristics. They tend to be more like one another than like the general population.[8] This introduces some unavoidable bias into any study. The group chosen by the DIS represented not just nuclear families and stepfamilies but also "research-friendly" adults who had enough stake in research about stepfamilies to volunteer.

By design, this study's sample was also carefully defined to control multiple variables. Only middle-class white families were studied. Stepfamilies were defined as stepfather families in which the mother had primary custody and the stepfather was a nonresidential parent. From the initial sample, a target population of forty-four children was identified for study. Over fifteen years of careful interviews, observation, and questionnaires, an immense body of information was gathered by top researchers.

---

[7]Bray and Kelly, *Stepfamilies.*

[8]R. Rosenthal and R. Rosnow, *The Volunteer Subject* (New York: Wiley, 1974). This study found that research volunteers tend to be better educated, have a higher social-class status, be more intelligent, have a higher need for social approval, be more sociable, be more arousal seeking, be more unconventional, be less authoritative, and be Jewish or Protestant than nonvolunteers. Volunteers are also more likely to be female than male.

Findings were interpeted and disseminated to scholars, clinicians, and the general population in journal articles and one popular stepfamily book.

The DIS study was an expensive, time-intensive, and lengthy project. It produced a great deal of information about stepfamilies. However, as the research team acknowledges, the study had clear limitations. It sampled a small number of people in one geographic area. Its subjects were all drawn from one small, highly specific socioeconomic, cultural, and racial population. It used measurement tools standardized on non-divorced people, and all subjects had some implicit or explicit stake in the outcome. Did we learn important things about stepfamilies from this study? Certainly. Can we use the study's results to develop new questions for further research? Yes. Can we use this data or its interpretation to make truth claims about all stepfamilies ? No. Can the conclusions of this study help us predict how any particular child or family will fare in stepfamily living? No. Can this study give us knowledge that will tell us with certainty why a stepfamily is in trouble or what they need? No. Good researchers know their limitations. Those who use research must do so carefully and tentatively.

CONTEXTUAL FACTORS

Inherent problems in the research task itself limit our trust that it can deliver truth about stepfamilies and their children. Several contextual problems increase our suspicion. Since the early 1900s, social sciences have assumed that the same rigorous scientific inquiry used in natural sciences could be used to establish laws that explain and predict human behavior. By separating theory from observation, inquiry could be neutral or value free. Tests, observations, measurements, and statistical analysis could prove or disprove any hypothesis. Adequate replication would allow truth claims grounded in the best of positivism. Prediction and control of human behavior would then be possible. These assumptions miss the fact that formal investigation takes place in a social and political environment. All research and all truth claims serve particular interests in local, cultural, and political struggles.[9]

The road from research to truth is not a simple linear process. Consciously or unconsciously, research participates in a recursive, reality-creating social discourse. It is not neutral. It is *for* someone. It is not value free; it is embedded in a historical context of value and meaning. Its facts are connected to values, and these facts cannot avoid being inducted into the dominant cultural ideology. The dominant culture, after all, asks research questions about things that stimulate its curiosity, abrade its values, or challenge its

[9]Laurel Richardson, "Writing: A Method of Inquiry," in *Handbook of Qualitative Research,* ed. Norman Denzin and Yvonna Lincoln (Thousand Oaks, Calif.: Sage, 1994), 517.

meanings. It is this culture that sets priorities for funding, determines acceptable methods for investigation, and defines criteria for truth. It teaches researchers what to observe and how. It orchestrates which findings will be published and what interpretation will be woven into knowledge and public policy. Mainstream research cannot help but participate in reproducing systems of class, race, and gender oppression as it asks questions, uses methods, frames findings, and produces knowledge in the language of dominant cultural ideologies.

Knowledge is power. It serves to undergird practices and policies that regulate what is considered reasonable and true. It also positions less privileged groups—such as stepfamilies—to accept their social status as natural, necessary, or inevitable. Because of generally accepted knowledge, people will act as if certain social or cultural relationships are true and will fail to notice blatant exceptions that challenge these truths. To notice the conflict would unsettle the structures of power and undermine the authority of the dominant group.[10] On the other hand, subordinate groups willingly avoid struggle by accepting their position. This collusion organizes life around limited truth and shrouds the political dimensions of everyday life in "common sense" knowledge that is immune to challenge. Consequently, stepfamilies are what the dominant culture assigns them to be. "Truth" about stepfamilies' experience is political and socially validated by knowledge that locks them into a subjugated position.

This process has concrete results. Language that organizes stepfamily experience and identity is formed around dominant truth, or nuclear family truth. Stepfamilies are what nuclear families are not. Researchers ask their questions against this defining foil: Children of divorce and remarriage deviate from the expected nuclear norm—what insufficiencies in their families or experience keep them from attaining the goods defined by this norm? Rarely is the norm itself questioned or stepfamily children's experience defined against its own context. An unassailable reality is created, formed against the mold of the dominant narrative and experience.

Research does not reveal impartial truth waiting to be uncovered by the appropriate archaeological tool or social science method. It actively helps construct culturally encapsulated "truths." Consider one example of how behavioral science research has colluded with cultural stereotypes.

Early in this century, psychological tests were developed to measure intelligence. In a few hours a psychologist could determine an individual's

---

[10]Joe Kincheloe and Peter McLaren, "Rethinking Critical Theory and Qualitative Research," in *Handbook of Qualitative Research,* ed. Norman Denzin and Yvonna Lincoln (Thousand Oaks, Calif.: Sage, 1994), 141.

intelligence quotient by asking a set of standard questions and observing a group of performance tasks. Over the years, intelligence was standardized. A group of norms emerged against which children and adults were measured in order to predict what could be expected of them in academic and vocational settings. I.Q. scores determined a child's school curricula, preferred placements, and vocational opportunities. Along the way, researchers noted that African Americans consistently scored lower on these tests than white Americans.

Research knowledge was used politically to validate dominant attitudes about African American deficiencies. First, it supported a theory proposed by G. Stanley Hall, the "father of child study" and the first president of the American Psychological Association. Based on research at the turn of the century, Hall postulated that Africans were an "adolescent race" that represented a lower stage of biological evolution. They were in a stage of incomplete development and could not be expected to perform equally with superior white races. Second, research with intelligence testing in the mid-1900s led social scientists to assert that Black, Mexican American, and other cultural minorities were genetically inferior and "uneducable." In the early 1970s, Stanford University's Nobel Prize-winning physicist William Shockley expressed fears that weak and low intelligence genes in the African American population would seriously affect overall intelligence in the United States. Heralded as a brilliant statistical analyst by Newsweek,[11] Shockley believed that unless certain white genes were added to the black population, African Americans were doomed to a dysgenic-retrogressive evolution. This view was supported by the University of California's respected educational psychologist Arthur Jensen.[12] By analyzing the variance in large numbers of intelligence tests, he concluded that African Americans as a population were genetically less intelligent than their white counterparts. As late as 1989, a professor at the University of Western Ontario presented research that claimed that human intelligence and behavior are determined by race. Whites have larger brains than Blacks, and Blacks are more aggressive than Whites, the professor said.[13]

Intelligence research also confirmed prevailing racial attitudes by contributing to a theory of cultural deficiency. Well-meaning social scientists proposed an alternative to genetic and evolutionary explanations of I.Q. differences. Racial minorities in the United States were culturally

---

[11]H. Simmons, "Is Intelligence Racial?" Newsweek, May 10, 1971, 69–70.

[12]Arthur Jensen, "How Much Can We Boost IQ and School Achievement?" Harvard Educational Review (1969): 1–123.

[13]Derald Sue and David Sue, *Counseling the Culturally Different* (New York: John Wiley & Sons, 1990), 18.

impoverished.[14] They lacked the education, adequate living space, books, toys, and formal language of white middle-class families. Inferior lifestyles undermined acceptable values, intelligence, and social skill development. The Moynihan Report,[15] presented in 1965, articulated a well-formed argument for cultural deficiency and advocated revising social policy to infuse white family values into African American homes. Cultural deprivation, a well-meaning argument explaining research-observed differences between dominant and subjugated populations, became an accepted political reality that pathologized people who were already living beyond the margins of the dominant culture.[16]

Research easily becomes a tool of prejudice that helps maintain the dominant cultural narrative. A "truth" was established: African American children, either because of bad genes or bad homes, could not be expected to fare as well academically as children from the dominant, white American culture. Research participated in reproducing class and racial oppression. Knowledge supported the dominant social truth. Like researchers observing "maze-smart" and "maze-dull" rats, teachers, schools, pastors, and others confirmed through "common sense" what research pointed out about culturally deprived children.

Though voices from the African American community questioned norms, protested how tests were constructed, and challenged the research upon which they were based, very little has changed since 1965. Subjugated voices have had little effect on educational or social policy. Attitudes about substandard minority homes and their effect on children are as deeply ingrained today as they were in the 1960s and 1970s. Kids from "culturally deprived" homes are still expected to fall short unless they are rescued into the dominant narrative. All research includes a political and economic stake, and some critics go so far as to suggest that the social sciences provide an especially effective vehicle for white, middle-class supremacy.

This example is relevant to stepfamilies who also are marginalized from the dominant cultural narrative. They are deviant and the target of much research. Like cultural minority children, their existence is a problem for entrenched institutional structures. Social theories, such as familism, try to explain these problems and the social distance between remarried and nuclear families. Stepfamilies have fallen from the evolutionary ladder that organizes and controls human sexual behavior. They must not be allowed to reproduce.

---

[14]F. Reissman, *The Culturally Deprived Child* (New York: Harper&Row, 1962).

[15]David Moynihan, "Employment, Income and the Ordeal of the Negro Family," *Daedalus* (1965): 745–70.

[16]S. Baratz and J. Baratz, "Early Childhood Intervention: The Social Sciences Base of Institutional Racism," *Harvard Educational Review* 40 (1970): 29–50.

Their marital and parental attachments are inferior, and they cannot be expected to produce the same quality of offspring as the nuclear family. Furthermore, they are culturally deprived, deficient, and disadvantaged. Because they lack the resources available to nuclear families, they cannot produce effective children or satisfactory family life. Divorce and remarriage is synonymous with family pathology. A self-fulfilling prophecy is set in motion that serves to maintain the status quo and to retain a political advantage for a dominant cultural group. Teachers expect lower grades, more behavioral pathology, and higher levels of dropouts because of children's "home situations." Children of divorce are problems who have problem parents. A non-abusing stepparent is an anomaly, and a stable stepfamily is an exception. If a child fails, becomes pregnant, drops out, or has a drug problem, we need look no further than their parents' divorce and remarriage. Happy stepfamilies, non-problem children, and functional young adults are invisible to observers and social policy makers guided by images of deprivation.

In fact, if we broaden our scope, few families of any form (nuclear, stepfamily, single-parent, etc.) consistently raise children with serious life-disrupting problems. Stepfamilies may have more than their share of the kinds of problems that irritate cultural values and gain institutional attention. They may have a hard time fitting into the dominant narrative. Even so, most stepfamilies produce well-functioning children and well-adjusted young adults.[17]

We see stepfamilies through a glass darkly. After nearly thirty years of research we know too much and too little about how children of divorce and remarriage fare. We know enough to produce experts who announce that stepfamilies are destroying children and a culture. One or two research studies can provide fragments of knowledge that experts exploit with great authority to tell stepfamilies how best to adjust and succeed. In their search for affirmation, stepparents and stepfamilies are often eager to invest in such "helps." On the other hand, our knowledge about children and remarriage is so slim that we are unable to interpret the many exceptions to the rule of stepfamily deficiency. Neither can we distinguish between what is genuinely helpful to stepfamilies and what infuses nuclear family values into "deficient" stepfamily households and makes them more culturally

---

[17]E. Hetherington, "The Role of Individual Differences in Family Relations in Coping With Divorce and Remarriage," in *Advances in Family Research: Vol. 2. Family Transitions,* ed. P. Cowan and E. Hetherington (Hillsdale, N.J.: Lawrence Erlbaum Associates, 1991); R. Emery "Parental Divorce and Children's Well-Being: A Focus on Resilience," in *Risk and Resiliency in Children,* ed. R. J. Haggerty, N. Garmenzy, M. Rutter, and L. Sherrod (London: Cambridge University Press, 1992); Hetherington and Jodl, "Stepfamilies as Settings for Child Development."

acceptable. Do healthy stepfamilies look any different than healthy nuclear families? Or is what we recognize as a healthy stepfamily simply a rewriting of a dominant cultural narrative on top of a subjugated stepfamily story? In truth, there is little evidence that expert advice arising from our limited knowledge has any impact on stepfamily well-being or child outcome.

Too often, stepfamily research is given undue authority to fix blame or give authoritative pronouncements of how stepfamilies fare. Things are simply not so clear, no matter how much we, or Dr. Laura, wish they were. Damning pronouncements based on limited research, whether uttered through the talk show lips of a radio personality or through public policy, are at best unhelpful. At worst, they can be damaging to people whose experience does not and cannot match the dominant cultural narrative.

Research and Pastoral Care

Research can be helpful, but it is not unqualified truth. Because it is such a trusted lens, information from research seeps powerfully into our discourse about stepfamilies and uncritically[18] into judgments framed by our dominant cultural narrative. Pastoral carers must exercise extreme care when using this information. We will need to evaluate our own biases. Is our agenda to support the dominant cultural narrative? Are we approaching stepfamily parents and children with nuclear expectations? Can we hear only what is familiar to us because it is part of a familiar nuclear family melody? Is difference the same as unacceptable deviance? Are we intending to embody a bias that stepfamilies are culturally or biologically inferior to nuclear families? Pastoral care that embodies the love of God will attend to these questions.

Listening to others' stories is integral to life in Christ. Pastoral listening to parents and children in remarried families must stay close to subjugated stories. It must be empathic enough to jar our sensibilities and press us into praxis. Embodied praxis will encourage critical dialogue with the full complexity of multiple voices that speak about stepfamily parents and children. Some of these will come from research. However, our beginning place is careful attention to what children and stepparents themselves tell us about their personal experience, their relationships with each other, and their relationships with institutions. The following chapter identifies some broad themes through which children's and parents' voices are heard.

---

[18]From the perspective of critical theory, this means information is accepted without clear evaluation of, or discourse about, the values, belief systems, ideologies, or historical contexts that undergird and are furthered by research findings. Critical evaluation would acknowledge research as a political act and take care to evaluate what persons and groups are enfranchised and disenfranchised.

Chapter 7
Stepfamilies, Children, and Parents

Tuning our Senses to Stepfamily Life

I began this book comparing stepfamily life to a wilderness journey walked without the aid of basic navigational tools. Most stepfamilies live without recognizable landmarks or any sure compass to point the way to safety and rest. Cultural exiles feel lost. Finding one's way daily through a foreign family landscape is disorienting. Stepfamilies spend their early years tentatively feeling their way around hazards, charging recklessly down impossible slopes, and struggling to free themselves from quicksand. Most new stepfamilies survive minute to minute, day to day, and crisis to crisis. Congregations and ministers must be willing to join stepfamilies in their wilderness and empower careful observation, informed exploration, and naming of the hazards that face the next step of the journey. This requires that congregations and pastoral carers tune their senses to a family's ecological context and attend to the voices, textures, temperatures, and interactions of stepfamily life in all its complexity.

During a recent workshop about stepfamilies and parenting, I was struck by the following exchange.

> **Elizabeth**: It's so hard being a stepparent to John's kids. I work all week and take care of my own kids. Then his kids show up every other weekend. I feel like I start over every time they visit. I have to remind them of the rules. I have to put up with their moods. I have to listen to John fume when they miss their mother. I have to change my whole family schedule because three more people are in the house.

Sarah: I know what you mean. My stepkids are with me every other weekend and one night a week. Even though they are there so often, it seems like they have no memory. They can't remember what the boundaries are or what's expected of them. And since they feel like visitors, they expect special treatment. My kids resent that. After their visits my kids will ask me for days why Allen's kids have to come so regularly. It disrupts their schedule and mine. At the same time, I feel sorry for Allen and his kids. It's got to feel bad when your father's home is a place you visit.

Jane: What I would give for your problems! Jerry's two kids live with us full-time. That makes five kids around all the time. There's no privacy, no space, and there's always conflict. I feel absolutely trapped most of the time. What I wouldn't give for a break! I love Jerry, but I hadn't planned on having his kids full-time. I'm not sure I would have married him had I known his ex-wife would move away and leave the kids behind. I'm tired. I feel the responsibility for all these kids all the time. Jerry does his share, but it's just not the same to be a stepdad as it is to be a stepmother. I get all the emotional baggage. I get all their moods. If they aren't satisfied, it's my fault. About half the time I just want to quit. It's going on three years now and some things have gotten better, but Lord, how I wish his ex-wife had stayed in town! (Laughs) I didn't think I would ever say that!

Erik: Jane, I hear your frustration. My kids don't live with me, and I miss them terribly. But I think it is easier that they don't. Our problem is a little more complicated. Lois got pregnant (probably) on our first anniversary celebration. Nine months later we had "hers," "mine," and "ours." Talk about ambivalence! Neither of us wanted a fourth child, at least not then.

By the time Jason was born, we were excited. Life had been chaotic, and we thought our own child would settle our relationship. You know, when everything is split between two families, you crave something that you've created together. Jason gave us some of that, but boy, life got crazy! We still haven't sorted out all the fear, feelings, and things between kids. I think everybody in the family was afraid Jason was going to upset something or take something away from somebody. Life was insane for almost two years. I don't know how we survived.

James: Wow! Another kid. I don't know what I would have done. Ellen and I had an understanding when we married. I'm the stepdad in the house. I don't have any authority except what she gives me. I can't do much with the kids except carry out what she wants. Even when my kids come to visit, I try not to upset the fruit basket. Ellen sets the rules, and I'll enforce them with my kids. I think that works for us. I do a lot of housework, but when it comes to kids, it's up to her. Even though Ellen sometimes complains she has too much responsibility for kids, she's clear that she wants the authority. That's fine with me. That's what we agreed to, and that's still what I want.

Jane: Jeez, James, it sounds like you have it made! I envy you. Jerry and I decided that our kids should have the benefit of two parents who were fully invested. Talk about hard work! It's been absolute chaos most of the time, but we worked hard at it. After almost four years, Jerry is a real parent to all of our kids. Most people who meet us are surprised that we're a stepfamily. Sure, sometimes one of my kids will yell at Jerry and tell him he's only my husband, not their dad. He seems to absorb that and does his dad thing. He's good at it. There are tense times, especially since my oldest is now 15. Truthfully, even though things are chaotic with four kids, I don't know that I'd trade how we did it.

Diversity and Common Ground

Stepfamilies can never be accused of being monotonous or too much alike. Every family has its unique character and its own style. However, in this diverse mix there are general structural themes around which stepfamilies tend to organize. One set of themes describes how the family is arranged around custody and who lives where. Another describes where and how adults place themselves as parents and spouses and where children fit in the scheme of everyday family life. Most remarried families will resonate best with one theme in each set.

Custody and residence themes. Custody and residence are primary organizing factors. Together they determine the daily tasks of stepfamily living and delineate a context for child, adult, and couple development.

- **Stepfather families** are the most common form of remarriage. In this arrangement, a husband either has no children or is a noncustodial parent whose children live with their mother. Studies show that these families are less stressful than other kinds of stepfamilies. Boys tend to respond more positively to these families than girls, though both frequently develop close and satisfying relationships with their stepfathers.
- **Stepmother families** are created when a father has custody of children that he brings into a marriage with a woman who has no children or is a noncustodial parent. These families tend to be more stressful than stepfather families, particularly for girls. Several strong dynamics may be at work to create problems for these families.[1]

---

[1] Emily Visher and John Visher, "Remarriage Families and Stepparenting," in *Normal Family Processes*, 2d ed., ed. Froma Walsh (New York: Guilford Press, 1993).

First, traditional cultural expectations dictate that women set the emotional tone for the family. Stepmothers are pressed to please stepchildren and produce harmony. When children are ungrateful, stepmothers internalize this as failure. Conflict then becomes personal and highly stressful. Second, the mother-daughter bond, which is disrupted when fathers gain custody, may be more upsetting to girls than when father-child bonds are disrupted. Stepfamily conflict seems to be more intense when it involves a noncustodial mother interacting with a stepfamily rather than a noncustodial father.

- **Complex stepfamilies**, in which both adults have residential children from a previous marriage, account for less than 10 percent of stepfamilies. These families are most likely of all stepfamilies to fail. There appears to be a direct correlation between the number of complex stepfamily children and redivorce. It is hard for both adults and children in these families to work out the complicated relationships inherent in this stepfamily form.[2]

- **Stepfamilies with a mutual child** comprise about half of remarried families. Stress increases greatly for couples who conceive early in stepfamily life. Those who are trying to bolster a failing marriage with a common child are often disappointed when their marriage becomes less, rather than more, stable. Children of previous marriages feel displaced and add stress to the marriage. The family undergoes more change in a short time, and new roles have to be negotiated. However, children born after a stepfamily has stabilized are likely to contribute positively to the family.[3]

Themes of child and parent roles and responsibilities. These themes describe how remarried couples choose to organize their households, roles, and responsibilities in order to meet daily life and developmental tasks.

- **Neotraditional stepfamilies** tend to remodel, or reconstruct, a nuclear family household. Couples who organize around this theme expect their marriage to provide a strong parental alliance with traditional forms of parental power and shared responsibility for child welfare. When neotraditional families work, they have high levels of cohesiveness and come close to being a "contemporary version of the

---

[2]LynnWhite and Alan Booth, "The Quality and Stability of Remarriages: The Role of Stepchildren," *American Sociological Review* 50 (1985): 689–98; A. Cherlin, "Remarriage as an Incomplete Institution," *American Journal of Sociology* 84 (1978): 634–50; E. Hetherington, "Coping with Family Transitions: Winners, Losers, and Survivors, Meetings of the Society for Research in Child Development," *Child Development* 60, no. 1 (1989): 1–14.

[3]Anne Bernstein, *Yours, Mine and Ours: How Families Change When Remarried Parents Have a Child Together* (New York: Scribners, 1989).

1950s white-picket-fence family."[4] These families appear to have found their way, at least partially, back into the dominant nuclear family narrative.

Creating this family is difficult. It depends on organizational strategies that minimize contact with ex-spouses and requires multiple levels of stepfamily cooperation. A couple must learn to support each other in parenting. Children must cooperate with parents and stepparents toward family ends in which they have minimal emotional investment. Neotraditional stepfamilies seem to benefit from nonresidential fathers' absence or marginal participation in their children's lives. Research suggests that many remarrying couples—particularly white, middle-class folk who have a historic stake in traditional nuclear family life—are likely to strive for this remarried family form.

- **Matriarchal stepfamilies** are characterized by a woman's dominant roles of wife and mother in the family. Frequently, these mothers have powerful personalities and clear domestic competence. Family leadership is the woman's responsibility. Usually, she is the custodial parent and makes most of the family's significant decisions. In matriarchal stepfamilies, a husband is interested primarily in his wife's companionship. He may take some parenting responsibility, but this is limited or peripheral. Since the couple relationship is separated from life with children, matriarchal husbands may or may not participate in family-centered activities. When a couple agrees about power and leadership, these stepfamilies are quite strong.[5]

- **Romantic stepfamilies** expect to reproduce a nuclear family immediately from the love and harmony based in the couple relationship. Their approach to stepfamily life, roles, and responsibilities is based on the unrealistic expectation that love will immediately conquer all the frustrations and chaos of divorce and remarriage. They want a traditional family, and they want it now. These stepfamilies are characterized by difficult stepparent-stepchild relationships, problems with former spouses, an inability to identify areas of disagreement, and marital failure. Romantic stepfamilies are more likely than either neotradional or matriarchal families to end in divorce.

How can attending to these themes help us see and hear stepfamilies? First, they point out that a stepfamily is not just a stepfamily. There are

---

[4]Bray and Kelly, *Stepfamilies*, 16.
[5]Ibid.

significant differences in style and organization. Second, they provide multiple lenses through which we can observe stepfamily process without qualitative judgment about how they compare to nuclear families. These are *stepfamily* themes, and they emerge from stepfamily experience. They do more than show differences between stepfamilies and nuclear families. Third, attending to these themes helps us listen more clearly to the specific voices of parents and children who live in stepfamilies. Listening for patterns helps us organize our perceptions and name experience more accurately. By opening our senses to both broad themes and individual voices, we can see the forest and appreciate individual characteristics of particular trees. Our job as pastoral carers is to be jarred. The more our senses are open to life in the wilderness, the more we will be touched by what happens around us. Even insensitive people are jarred by a forest fire that destroys millions of acres and threatens their homes. Only those who live in the forest or have an intimate relationship with it are awake to changes in one tree, or an affliction borne only by one species of bird. This kind of specific attention and knowledge provides a point of contact for embodied ministry.

Seeing Patterns and Hearing Melodies

When we left Larry and Sharon Willis in chapter 5, their stepfamily dynamics had produced intense stress that threatened the couple's marriage and the family's survival. Recalling a few details, we can identify the Willis family as a complex, romantic stepfamily. Both Larry and Sharon brought residential children to their union. Both expected to recreate a nuclear family almost immediately. Larry, in particular, was frustrated and angry when his expectation of "instant love" did not materialize with Sharon's children. Sharon was more realistic, but she also expected her new family to fit quickly into familiar traditional roles. The couple insisted on traditional parent-child roles and shared parental authority. Symptoms developed as children faced impossible demands to accommodate their parent's wish for a happy, traditional, two-parent home. Larry and Sharon, in their desire to coalesce a complex family quickly, did not understand the changes and challenges their children faced . Both parents and children were overcome by complex stressors. What happened in their family highlights several experiences common for children and parents in stepfamilies.

Children's Voices

Children's stepfamily stories are especially complex. They must manage myriad changes and have little power over their own lives and futures. They also live with parents who are caught in the sticky web of new, stress-filled roles where old rules no longer work. Young voices are likely be missed, or at least misheard, during the early years of stepfamily life. To complicate matters, most children are developmentally unable to form thoughts and sentences to express intense emotional experiences. In remarried families, children who can verbalize their experience often do not. There are consequences for such honesty. Instead, children express their deepest emotions through their actions in families and among their primary communities. By listening to children's and adolescents' stories through their behavior and words, we can see the shape of children's experience in stepfamilies.

Larry Willis' daughter, Mary, was the "quietest" child in the new stepfamily. She was well behaved and seemed to have few problems associated with divorce and remarriage. Yet if we listen to her behavior, two important messages from stepfamily children become clear.

As the wedding approached, ten-year-old Mary began daydreaming about her mother. She told her father that she missed Mom and wished that their whole family could "just go home." She missed their old house, the dog she had to leave behind, and her friends. After almost a year in their new home, she still had no friends. Larry reassured Mary that all would be well. Remarrying would make their new house feel more like a home. Sharon would be a good "mom-figure" for when she felt bad. He reminded Mary that she could not go "back to their home." That house had been sold, the furniture was all gone, and her mom was living with someone else. He promised she would soon be comfortable in their new family home. Mary seemed satisfied.

The following three months were a rush of wedding, moving, and trying to get everyone settled. Mary stayed in her room most of the time, especially as conflict erupted between her brother and Jon. She often complained to Larry about stomach cramps at bedtime, but antacids helped. When Mary cried and did not want to go to school because of a stomachache, Larry became concerned. A brief medical examination reassured Larry that nothing was wrong with Mary. "Some kids are school phobic. They'll do what they can to manipulate parents into letting them stay home," counseled the doctor. He was more concerned with Mary's weight gain. His prescription was more parental control of her eating and school attendance. Larry insisted, and Mary went to school. After this episode, Mary cried each night as she went to bed. When Larry asked her why, she replied, "I miss Mommy." Nights when Sharon put her to bed, Mary withdrew, turned her back on Sharon, and closed her eyes.

As conflict with Bryan worsened, Larry's concern with Mary faded until her first grade report. Her usual A's had become low C's and one D. Her teacher reported no behavior problems. Mary needed to try harder, get her homework done on time, and concentrate while taking tests. The teacher was concerned that Mary had few friends at school.

Sharon was home more, so she took responsibility for Mary's homework. After two weeks, she complained to Larry that she had no authority. Mary would not cooperate. That evening, Larry and Sharon met with the children. Mary and Drew were told that they would now call Sharon "Mom" because she was "the mom of this house." Jon was told he would call Larry "Dad." Since Bryan was older, he could call Larry by his first name. The next evening Mary refused to do her homework and exclaimed to Sharon, "You're not my mom!" She locked herself in her room. Sharon responded by assigning Mary extra chores because of her outburst and uncooperative behavior. Mary complied and then retired to her room. Her grades were no better at the end of the school term.

While children's experience in early stepfamily life is complex and confusing, Mary's behavior highlights the importance of recirculating grief and accumulating stress for children who live in stepfamilies.

Recirculating grief. It is easy to interpret reticence, withdrawal, behavioral regression to a younger age, and "crankiness" as a child's willful resistance to adult expectations. Larry and Sharon saw Mary's refusal to do her homework, her daydreaming, and her outburst as defiance of her stepmother's authority. In his romantic enthusiasm to recapture a new nuclear family through remarriage, Larry missed his daughter's statement of grief. He dismissed the sadness and tragedy of Mary's longing for her mother, her old house, and her dog. Instead, he tried to enlist her into his own romantic stepfamily vision. His injunction was to deny feelings of loss. Mary should "get over" the reality that her old life was gone. She should move on to her new life and family. This was impossible, and Mary was left alone with her multiple losses. She was never told that all children of divorce grieve. Neither could her father share her feelings of loss or help her reconnect to those things she would always have from her family of origin. Instead, his own unresolved anger and unrealistic, romantic expectations clouded his vision.

Mary was pressed to deny her own experience and to collude with a new romantic family vision. Unwilling to risk losing her father, she did not rebel against his enthusiasm. Instead, Mary chose to disappear. She withdrew to her room, disengaged from her school, and complied at almost every turn. When sorrow did erupt, she quickly conformed to adult authority and became invisible. Adults noticed only her physical complaints. Her poor school performance and resistance to change were interpreted as disobedience. Mary's symptoms were not disruptive enough for teachers or parents to be overly concerned about her sadness or grief. Her physician noted her weight gain but did not question loss, grief, or changes in her life.

Children's grief in divorce and remarriage can be hard to see or be misplaced amid the clutter of adult concerns and parents' guilt. Yet recognizing, responding to, and managing recapitulating grief in a new stepfamily is critical. These families, after all, grow *through* grief, not in spite of it. To disregard children's behavioral responses to loss and change will quickly escalate stepfamily turbulence.

Accumulated stress. As Mary's story shows, grief plays a large part in children's stepfamily drama. This is not a solo performance. The same stressors that undermine newly remarried couples have serious implications for children and stepfamily life.

Most children are remarkably resilient. However, divorce and remarriage expose children to multiple long-term stressors. Children in divorcing families endure extended periods of parental conflict. At separation, they are forced to adjust to single-parent living and the absence of a non-custodial parent. Most learn to live with fewer economic resources, disrupted parental styles, chaotic household routines, and uncertain status in school, church, and community. When parents remarry, children's family structure and relational field shift again. Most change homes; some change schools. Early in stepfamily life they must acclimate to a host of new people and relationships. All have to manage the conflict and disequilibrium of turbulent family reorganization.

Multiple stressors threaten a child's need for safety, security, and predictability. Like any group of children who live with chronic multiple stressors, stepfamily children are at risk for behavioral, emotional, and physical problems.[6] How an individual child responds to stress is highly variable and depends on her or his internal and external resources. Some children are stress-adaptive by temperament and, with good support, suffer few problems. Others with low immunity to stress may develop severe symptoms that demand immediate intervention. Stepfamily children fill the continuum between these two poles.

Mary Willis was a child at risk. Her parents' divorce was conflict-filled and extended over many months. Neither she nor her brother were protected from her parents' mutual animosity. Though many of her parents' arguments were child-centered, she and Drew were overlooked. Larry and Pam expended all their energy and resources on the last gasping breath of their marriage. The children listened as their parents disparaged each other to friends and discounted the other parent's rules and decisions. At divorce,

---

[6]E. Hetherington, Margaret Stanley-Hagan, and Edward Anderson, "Marital Transitions: A Child's Perspective," *American Psychologist* 44 (1989): 303–12.

Mary was forced suddenly and completely to move from the only home she had known. Two weeks later, she entered a new school where she had no friends. Her new home included more responsibility for household chores and "taking care of dad." When Larry started dating, Mary had to adjust to seeing less of her father and sharing him with another woman. Larry and Sharon's marriage initiated a new set of adjustments.

More than two years of rapid and frequent change depleted Mary's considerable ability to manage stress. Because she was quiet and competent, adults overlooked how stress affected her. However, she began to collapse when she met the first turbulent cycle of stepfamily life. Jon, Drew, and Bryan's problems drew focus and support away from her. Her academic and physical symptoms were normalized by her teacher and a physician. Mary's competence joined with Larry and Sharon's romantic denial, and she became a disobedient child rather than one folding under excessive stress and extended grief. Instead of a compassionate response, Mary's symptoms reaped higher expectations backed by firm consequences. Her stress increased, and she was hurt by her own ability to manage stress well.

The children in Mary's family reacted differently to stress and grief. Jon regressed to behavior and attitudes of a much younger child. Drew became aggressive, irritable, and territorial. All four children's school performance suffered. Bryan was most affected. Not only did he carry multiple stressors of divorce and remarriage, he also suffered a collision with adolescence at the same time his mother remarried. His familiar landscape disappeared, and his new stepfamily could not support the chaos of his transition. This fired such intense conflict that he became self-destructive as his emotional, cognitive, and social systems collapsed. With their romantic approach to remarriage, Larry and Sharon could not see how their unrealistic expectations and stepfamily stressors colluded with Bryan's collapse. Because of his outrageous behavior, Bryan easily garnered credit for his stepfamily's disintegration.

Stepfamily children are more likely than other children to accumulate stress. As Mary's case points out, chronic stress and unresolved grief can become fused in these children, especially during the first two years of stepfamily life. Grief becomes a primary stressor, and stress-inducing changes increase loss and grief. Together, these rob children of their vitality and their resources to manage daily life. When children suffer symptoms, a couple's relationship is compromised and the stepfamily is at risk for failure. It is critical that pastoral carers find ways to attend to both subtle and florid messages that children are being overwhelmed by grief and stress.

Conflicting loyalties. Bryan's story, told through his behavior, highlights conflicting loyalties as a third theme common to children's experience in stepfamilies. This force, which drives a couple's conflict, is more toxic to children. Let's consider parts of Bryan's story that were not told in chapter 5.

> Bryan was born just after Sharon and Pete's first anniversary. Both of them wanted a child, and Pete was overjoyed that his first was a son. He had been close to his own father. Together they hunted and fished and enjoyed all the sports available in their rural community. Pete looked forward to his relationship with Bryan. His only regret was that it would take several years before Bryan "got interesting." From age six until his parents' divorce when he was eleven, Bryan had Pete's active attention. Father and son hunted and fished together. Pete coached Bryan's Little League football team. One of Pete and Sharon's early conflicts was about Pete's drinking when Bryan was with him on outings. Sharon saw Bryan as a sensitive boy who desperately wanted a relationship with his father. She believed Pete pushed him too hard. Bryan would do anything to please him, including sidestep his own feelings and imitate his father's bad habits.
>
> When Pete and Sharon divorced, Sharon limited Bryan's contact with Pete. She was convinced Pete was drinking too much and worried that he would be as emotionally abusive to Bryan as he was to her. Pete responded by refusing to pay child support or see the children regularly. Sharon remembered his comment, "You think I'm so bad for them, then just do it all on your own." Nevertheless, Pete continued to take Bryan hunting several times a year, always came to his school games, and was beginning to teach his now fifteen-year-old son how to drive. When Pete heard about Sharon's plan to remarry, his comment to Bryan was, "Well, I hear your mom's got a new bed partner. Don't forget who your father is."

Bryan's story highlights the toxic impact of intense loyalty conflict. For nearly five years, Bryan survived parental conflict in which he was central. To be with his father meant he betrayed his mother. To be with his father augmented his angry grief that his mother had left the marriage and limited his contact with Pete. He frequently was forced to choose which parent to please. Since Sharon supported him and provided his home, he most often chose to side with her. He loved both his mother and father and did not understand why they could not get along. Bryan faced an impossible choice.

Sharon's remarriage fueled more loyalty conflicts. Larry expected Bryan to welcome his overtures as a paternal replacement. After all, Pete was an incompetent father. He failed to support his children and spent little time with them. Larry believed Bryan had a weak paternal attachment that would be healed by Larry's willingness to recreate a nuclearlike family inclusive of Bryan and Jon. He was wrong. By moving quickly to fill in for Pete, Larry ignited the flame of Bryan's attachment to his father. He immediately dismissed Larry and resented his mother for forcing another "father" on him. Bryan's oppositional behavior and drinking became a living attachment to his father. At one point Bryan remarked, "I guess I take after my dad." He met Larry's comments that he was "just like Pete" with pride.

Sharon's remarriage and romantic stepfamily vision gave Bryan few options. Loyalty to his father meant he must reject his mother's choices. What relief there might have been in being a son to both his divorced parents was lost when Sharon insisted he be a son only to Larry. Bryan was trapped. By rejecting Larry's instant parenthood, he rejected Sharon's authority. It was, after all, at her insistence that Bryan became Larry's son. To obey Sharon meant rejecting his relationship with his father. When Larry insisted on full parenthood and authority, the fire of Bryan's conflicting loyalties exploded.

Sharon too was caught in this trap. If she questioned Larry's parenting position with Bryan, she challenged the very foundation of their relationship. The couple's commitment was to a reconstruction of what they had lost. On the other hand, if she stood with Larry's parenting authority and their mutual vision of marriage, she lost her son to stress- and grief-related symptoms.

Perhaps the most common form of conflicting loyalties is found in the "insider/outsider gap."[7] The fact that every stepfamily is a merger of two or more families creates tension. When only one spouse brings residential children to remarriage, strong parent-child biological ties often isolate the stepparent who does not. This dynamic undermines couple development and impacts stepparent-stepchild relationships. In stepfather families, the mother-child bond is often "an impenetrable biological force-field."[8] Since a stepfather cannot relate to either mother or child the way they relate to each other, he often feels powerless and lives in relative isolation. Wives are cheated out of husbands, and children forfeit strong attachment to stepfathers. When the insider/outsider gap persists, tension and conflict permeate the family system. Men, women, and children feel the pinch of competing loyalties. Family cohesion becomes impossible. A primary developmental task early in stepfamily life is to bridge this chasm.

Conflicting loyalties are a powerful fact in remarried families. They symbolize the tragedy of lost marriages and provide a metaphor for multiple injustices. Often, it is this dull knife that eviscerates stepfamily emotional processes and aborts the possibility of new stepparent-stepchild ties.

---

[7]Bray and Kelly, *Stepfamilies*, 122 ff.
[8]Ibid., 124.

As stepfamilies interact in congregational settings, it is critical that pastoral carers attend to conflicting loyalties played out in religious rituals and activities. In an interview, twenty three-year-old Duane recalled the intense conflict that surrounded his most significant religious rite:

I was only seven. Both my parents were active Baptists. Since my parents had joint custody of me, I went to church with both of them. One week I'd go with my mom, the following week with my dad. My mom remarried pretty soon after her divorce, so every other week I went to church with her and her new husband. My mom wanted me to be baptized. I was pretty young, but I think I understood what it was all about. The pastor asked if I knew Jesus as my savior, and I said yes. He asked if I wanted to be baptized. Truthfully, I just wanted to please my mom, so I said yes. They set the schedule, and I was baptized two weeks later. I didn't tell Dad, and my mom didn't tell Dad. When I was baptized, he was not there. It was like I had to keep everything separate. I was really terrified my dad would find out. I knew he would be upset. Religion was really important to him, and he had talked about how he wanted to be part of my baptism. I was afraid and felt guilty about Mom's having me baptized. But I also felt like I couldn't do anything about it. It was pretty schizophrenic.

Sure enough, my sister slipped and told Dad. He cried. I felt awful, like I had betrayed him. Later that night the phone rang, and I heard him talking to the pastor of the church. He was really angry and reamed the guy out for not checking to see if what Mom had said about him was true—that he wasn't interested. That left a really bad taste in my mouth. I just wanted to go back and get un-baptized. I've grown up, and I don't feel much like being part of the church. I still won't take communion, and I want to leave when I know someone is being baptized. I should want to be part of the church. It was so important to my parents, and even to me at times. But I get really put off by religious things.

Honoring the fact that children in remarried families have nonresidential biological ties is critical for all dimensions of congregational life if stepfamily reality is to be honored.

The pressure of conflicting loyalties moves vertically from child to parents. It also moves horizontally as couples struggle with loyalty to their new spouses and to their biological commitment to their children. Most successful stepfamilies also wrestle with oblique loyalty conflict as stepparents begin to attach to stepchildren.

At age forty-eight Lloyd became a stepfather to eleven year-old Stacie. His own two children were away at college, and he and Julie established a matriarchal stepfather stepfamily. For the first year of marriage, Lloyd had minimal contact with Julie's young daughter. However, as his relationship with Julie strengthened, he found himself enjoying contact with Stacie.

After two years of marriage, he was surprised by Stacie's obvious attachment to him and his own affection for her. In fact, he was frightened by his feelings. He felt guilty about resources he now had for Stacie that were unavailable when his own nonresidential children were young. This was exacerbated when his twenty-year-old daughter discovered he drove Stacie to school. She was furious. How could he do such things for his stepdaughter when she had missed so much because of divorce? Lloyd wrestled with his developing love for Stacie, which seemed disloyal to his own children. How could he give to her what his own children had lacked? Worse was the fact that he could not go back and change history for his daughter.

This is a common conflict for stepparents. It is impossible to develop stepfamily intimacy without confronting tension about what belongs to stepchildren and to biological children. This conflict is rooted in what proponents of critical familism refer to as kin altruism. They observe that evolutionary necessity predisposes us to give the best to our own offspring and neglect stepchildren with whom we have no biological tie. Don Browning, David Popenoe, and other advocates of critical familism identify this as a "male problematic." Kin altruism is the fundamental biological and social mechanism established by evolution that motivates men to invest in their own genetic survival (and, consequently, survival of the species) by protecting women and protecting children who are guaranteed to carry their genes. Without this filial mandate, there is little reason for a man to invest deeply in parenting or make sacrifices for women or children. Since most children of divorce live in stepfather families with a custodial mother, this theory has strong implications for the quality of parenting in stepfamilies.

This argument from biology and evolutionary psychology is used powerfully to support the proposition that stepfamilies are inadequate environments for child-rearing. It is a limited and pessimistic view of the human person. By discounting both men's and women's ability to transcend the social limitations imposed by biological history, it focuses human meaning in evolutionary forces and species survival. This presents a paradox because critical familism (and Western Christianity) expects men and women to transcend the biological mandate to reproduce at will, and instead live for meanings and values rooted in monogamy.[9] This requires commitment

---

[9]The argument by evolutionary psychology that monogamy is a cultural adaptation to better ensure species survival is a speculative anthropological stretch that places moral vision, ethical behavior, and human self-transcendence behind genetic mandate.

and self-transcendence and is expected to be possible. Why is self-transcendence in stepparenting any less possible or more remote an obligation? It is at this point that the gospel of Christ can be embodied in stepfamilies. Jesus the Christ is God's symbol of inclusive love that breaks the boundaries of biology, culture, social history, and kin altruism. The church—the body of Christ—is charged with living out God's message of inclusive love, which expands grace, relational meaning, and care beyond usually acceptable limits. It extends it to those who normally would be excluded. This is hope for stepparents and stepchildren living together under the cloud of conflicting loyalties and expectations of kin altruism.

Without close, affectionate ties with stepparents, stepchildren are cheated. They will not receive the benefit of genuine grace or balanced love. Stepparent-stepchild relationships without affection are stereotyped, ritualized activities that lack the flexibility or care that undergirds healthy, successful families. In congregational life, stepfamilies need constant reminders of God's incarnate love at work in them, which can transcend boundaries, expand grace, and break the limits of filial hegemony. This message must be present in all dimensions of religious life that touch stepfamilies. However, it is likely to be heard only in congregations able first to make room for stepfamilies to express the painful dilemmas of conflicting loyalties and then to embody a destabilizing gospel that upsets conventional wisdom, turns expectations upside down, and redeems the unlikely. When stepchild-stepparent relationships are redeemed and conflicting loyalties well managed, they embody a picture of God's multi-dimensional, inclusive love that transcends all usual boundaries. This in itself may be stepfamilies' greatest contribution to life in the body of Christ.

Parenting, discipline, and setting boundaries. Loyalty conflicts, stressors surrounding change, and recapitulating losses surface painfully in stepparent-stepchild role negotiation. This mutual adjustment between stepparents and stepchildren is a difficult task. It is also the task that determines a stepfamily's temperament and success. In families where mutual adjustment and effective role negotiation are successful, children are less anxious about loyalty conflicts and are less likely to suffer ill effects from stress. Satisfied children, after all, seem to be foundational for well-adjusted remarried couples and effective stepfamilies.

No matter how well a couple has prepared, most stepfamilies begin with deep ambivalence about step-relationships and step-roles. Merging two families into one household disrupts even the best-laid plans. Although good marital preparation helps a couple keep their expectations about stepfamily life realistic, no amount of advance planning can equip children and parents for the real-life experience of stepping into the remarriage crucible. Rational forethought is quickly challenged by the irrational emotional spirits loosed when a remarried family combines households. At deep, pre-verbal levels, children wonder, *Who is this new adult who now sleeps with Mom (or Dad) and takes up room in this house? Who is he (or she) to me?* At more conscious levels, children question why rules formed in single-parent families have to change because of new stepparents to adapt to stepfamily living.

Ten-year-old Beth came to a counseling session with her parents and two younger brothers. Her mother, Alice, had married James two months before their first session. Alice initiated counseling because she wanted "everything to go right" as the stepfamily formed. Beth's responses highlight how children often experience adjustments to new stepfamilies.

Counselor: Beth, what do you think has changed since your mom and James got married?

Beth: Well, James stays overnight now and sleeps with Mom. (Pause)

Counselor: Have you noticed any other changes?

Beth: Yeah. Sometimes James tells me what to do, and sometimes he takes me to school in the morning. He gets in the way a lot.

Counselor: What do you mean?

Beth: When I want to talk to Mom, he's there all the time. When I want to watch TV, he's already there and I have to watch what he's watching.

Counselor: It sounds like there are some good things and bad things...you know, like he takes you to school, and he gets in the way. What do you think some good things are?

Beth: It's nice to have a bigger house now and a nicer car. Sometimes James gives me money when Mom won't. When he picked me up from school last week, we stopped for ice cream. I liked that.

Counselor: Are there some bad things too?

Beth: Yeah. Kinda. (Looks at Mom, who nods that it is all right to speak. Mom says, "Honey, we're here to be honest about our feelings.") Well...(pause) I don't like it when James tells me what to do. Mom's at home and she should do that. I liked the rules we had before James got here. We didn't have to clean up as much, and we didn't have to do chores. Now James makes us do chores and stuff. It kinda makes me mad when he tells me what to do.

Counselor: Hmmm. Are there other things that make you mad?

Beth: (Looks at her mom, who smiles and encourages her to go on.) Well, it's kinda like I hate it when I break a rule and James makes me go to my room.

Counselor: What do you feel when that happens?

Beth: I wish he'd leave, go find his own kids to punish. Just 'cause he's older than Mom and his kids are older, he thinks he knows all about how kids feel and how they should act. I want things to go back the way they were when it was us and Mom.

Beth's experience is not unusual. Most children can see both the good and hard parts of gaining a new stepparent. Few would willingly trade their single-parent home for a stepfamily, regardless of the economic advantage. As a rule, stepchildren do not want a new parent, even though most remarrying couples *want* their children to want a new parent figure. This complicates budding stepparent-stepchild relationships.

By using the counseling process in the first years of marriage, Beth's mother and new stepfather were able to consider thoughtfully how they would bridge the insider/outsider gap and become stepparents. Unlike the Willises, Alice and James knew that stepfamily life would be hard. They believed it was important to nurture their own relationship and form roles with children that would work over the "long haul." They willingly (if not happily) put off immediate couple and parental gratification in order to anticipate future success. Their counselor encouraged them to move slowly and to set priorities. First, they needed to evaluate how fast change in their new family should happen. The couple had implemented one or two sweeping household changes in their first month together, and the children had reacted badly. Children, their counselor suggested, may be resilient and flexible, but too much change can overtax any child. The new couple agreed to make changes one at a time. They would wait to see what result one change had before adding to it or altering any other household procedure. James agreed to put some of his own needs about an organized household off for a while so that the children's adjustment away from single-parent routines could slow down.

Second, Alice and James explored what they wanted in stepparent-stepchild relationships. Alice wished for a full parenting partner but realized this was unrealistic. Her children were resistant to the idea of James's acting as a parent. She also found herself uneasy with James's attempts to get close to the children or to take much responsibility and authority with them. She loved James, but these were not his children, and she did not fully trust his parental judgment. Someday this would change, but for now it was simply a fact.

James wanted a good relationship with Alice's children. He also felt he had no real authority with them and readily admitted he did not want equal responsibility for them. Together the counselor and couple explored the fact that the only authority *any* stepparent has is derivative—it is derived from whatever authority the biological parent can give to the stepparent without sharp or obvious ambivalence. This was fine with James, who acknowledged his own ambivalence. Since his children did not live with him, he wanted to reserve some parenting "just for them." He and Alice determined that the best way to manage this was for James not to become a disciplinarian quickly. Instead, he would befriend Alice's children and take responsibility for backing up Alice on parenting decisions. He would provide physical support, such as transportation and helping children with homework when needed. However, rules for the children would come from Alice. Alice would have the added bonus of a benevolent "second set of eyes" watching out for her children. James and Alice agreed they wanted more mutuality as parents in the future but knew this would develop over years.

In counseling, the couple also made agreements about how Alice would parent James's children when they visited. She too would take things slowly with James's teenage daughters. When they visited, he would have to be home most of the time. He would set rules and enforce them. Any disagreement Alice had about visitation would be directed to James when the girls were not present. She had no desire to become an evil stepmother. The couple agreed to talk about what worked and did not work the day after each visitation. Any topic too hot to talk about without serious conflict could be tabled until their next counseling session.

As Alice and James neared the end of two years of marriage, they saw their agreements pay off. Neither had received all they wanted from marriage, but both were satisfied. Their journey had been hard. They had nearly separated several times over parenting disagreements. Mostly these were related to one of them feeling helpless with the other's children. As they looked back, they realized they were competent stepparents and comfortable in their roles. Alice still took primary responsibility for her children and enforced most of the household rules. James had discovered nonreactive ways to set boundaries that mattered to him with Alice's children. He also found that his stepchildren were attached to him. This allowed him to tolerate their moods, anger, and misbehavior without becoming reactive. Alice accomplished many of these same tasks with James's children. A conversation with twelve-year-old Beth after two years highlights positive change.

> **Counselor:** Well, Beth, it's been a long time since we first met. What's it like to live in a stepfamily now?
>
> **Beth:** Well, you know, its kinda like I don't remember it any other way. We just live together.
>
> **Counselor:** Do you think you are like other families, or different?
>
> **Beth:** I dunno. A lot of my friends live in stepfamilies. Some of them hate 'em; some don't think too much about it. So, I dunno. I guess I don't think too much about it any more.
>
> **Counselor:** When we first talked, I asked you what was good and what was bad about your stepfamily. Can you answer that now?
>
> **Beth:** I guess. I guess I'm kinda used to it. We get along pretty good now.
>
> **Counselor:** Does James still tell you what to do?
>
> **Beth:** Oh, yeah, all the time (smiles at James). Mom leaves a list, and he tells me what to do. He reminds me what will happen if I don't do what's on the list. Sometimes, when I'm in trouble, though, he'll talk Mom out of really grounding me or taking away my telephone for a whole week. 'Course, they don't think I know that.
>
> **Counselor:** It seems like when we first met, you felt like James was always in the way. Do you still feel that way?
>
> **Beth:** Oh, yeah! But so's Mom. They're always in my way. They always want the telephone, or the TV. They're always wanting me to go do some dumb family thing.
>
> **Counselor:** Is that okay?
>
> **Beth:** No, but I guess I'm stuck with it.
>
> **Counselor:** Well, how about when James's kids come to visit?
>
> **Beth:** They're only here in the summer, and it's kind of neat to have teenagers around. I get to do more stuff since they're older.

Alice and James met with a counselor monthly for almost two years. When they terminated the sessions, they had forged a mutual vision for their family, survived much of the turmoil of early stepfamily life, and formed a good sense of being "together." By successfully managing changes, conflicting loyalties, and changing roles associated with merging two families, Beth's "him and us" shifted to a strong sense of "we." Her "us-them" split now related more to an adolescent's demanding more space from parents who were holding her captive than to biological and nonbiological parental connections.

James and Alice recalled how difficult it was for their family to create new cohesion-building rituals. Bringing their families together actually meant that six sets of family rituals had to be respected and integrated into their new life. Both James and Alice had rituals from their own families of origin, from their previous marriages, and from their single-parent families. The couple was intentional about keeping some rituals from earlier families that nourished biological parent-child ties. They also worked hard to create rituals that symbolized their new family life. Together they established a weekly movie night, a parent date night, after-church pizza on the Sundays they were all together, and an annual vacation shared by all children and stepchildren in the family. Though Alice felt that "alien forces" tried to keep them from being consistent, after two years their children called them to account when necessity dictated change in their new family rituals.

Cycles and seasons. The Developmental Issues in the StepFamilies Research Project (DIS)[10] found that stepfamilies live through three broad developmental cycles. The first two-year period is marked by turbulence as the family negotiates mergers and conflicts that accompany remarriage. During this cycle, remarried couple's hopes and expectations are challenged and transformed. This is a troubling and dangerous time for stepfamilies as painful divorce and remarriage dilemmas are felt in their raw, unmitigated force. Redivorce and stress symptoms are most common during this first cycle.

The second cycle of stepfamily life is a three- to five-year "golden period" in which the dividing points and turmoil of cycle one are mostly resolved. Alice's family at the end of counseling is an example of a stepfamily entering this second cycle. The DIS Project observed that significant shifts take place between cycle one and two. Children's behavioral problems decrease markedly when a stepfamily enters the second cycle of life together. Reduced problems for children have direct, positive consequences for remarried couples. The study measured rates of stress for parents and stepparents, and found these rates decrease by nearly 200 percent as families enter cycle two.

Romantic stepfamilies were exceptions to this pattern. Their unwillingness to relinquish unrealistic expectations keep them in revolving cycles of stress and turmoil. As a group, romantic families cannot accept one stepfamily fact: Remarried families have permeable boundaries. Ex-spouses, nonresidential stepchildren, and a variety of other folk have access to stepfamilies in ways foreign to the nuclear families they are trying to

---

[10]Bray and Kelly, *Stepfamilies*, 183.

reproduce. Matriarchal and neotraditional stepfamilies are more able to accept and adapt to this reality. Romantic stepfamilies stay bound to cycle one because they insist on a "just us" posture that locks out all intruders. This is not possible, and romantic stepfamilies suffer.

A third stepfamily cycle emerges in years five through nine. By this time, many stepfamilies are enduring their children's passage to adolescence. Stepfamily life is mostly good and getting better. The eruption of adolescence in one or more children, however, reignites certain conflicts. Children's behavior and social problems reemerge. Unlike cycle one, these outbreaks are associated with teenage transitions rather than divorce and remarriage.

Paradoxically, remarried couples in the third cycle of stepfamily life actually reported an increase in marital satisfaction. Researchers suggested that weathering the intense trials of cycle one without losing hope provided a solid stepfamily identity. This drew couples together in common concern for impossible adolescents and their life together. "Us and them" had given way to "our family" and its concerns. Increased marital satisfaction in the third cycle of stepfamily life also reflected a sense of shared pride and achievement. Together the couple survived stepfamily turmoil and an intolerable adolescent. Most cycle three stepfamilies also saw positive results of their life together as their launched children became successful in college, vocation, and social life.

Stepfamilies are capable of strong family commitments. They can provide the resources needed for effective family outcomes. To be of help, pastoral carers, counselors, and remarried parents must attend to the critical developmental and emotional issues of recirculating grief, debilitating stress, conflicting loyalties, and cohesion earned through stepfamily life cycles.

Themes for Theology and Pastoral Care

Constructing a remarried family that can sustain child and adult development takes time and the ability to contain anxiety and conflict. Remarried families who attract a congregation's attention are most often in their first cycle of stepfamily life. They are bound in conflict and anxiety. They are unable to coalesce or adjust to critical stepparent-stepchild tasks. These situations present the most formidable pastoral-care problems. Families in the second and third cycles of stepfamily life may need care, but do not usually carry the same weight of explosive potential. No matter where a stepfamily is developmentally, responding with care to children and parents requires careful attention to emotional and relational realities unique to stepfamilies. A guiding theological frame must embrace them as worthwhile and part of God's redemptive narrative.

Strong religious and political voices doubt that stepfamilies belong in a redemptive moral vision or are a worthwhile context for family life. They say stepfamilies are part of a destructive cultural influence, that remarried families threaten the family as a social institution and imperil individual children. This argument rests on three broad assumptions:

- Divorce is bad and destructive.
- Research proves that stepfamilies are detrimental to children, are likely to raise young adults with multiple academic, vocational, and social problems, and predispose subsequent generations to reproduce divorced families.
- Evolution of the human species argues against stepfamilies. Men and women who do not have biological ties to offspring are either incapable of or unlikely to love and care for children who are not their own.

Few thinking folk can argue with the first assumption. Divorce, as Jesus pointed out, is a result of hard hearts. It can be nothing other. Divorce symbolizes one or more people's choosing self-interest at another's expense. This is true whether an abusive husband creates a home incapable of sustaining life, or a couple agrees to end their marriage because individual needs cannot be fulfilled completely by marriage. Divorce is violence. It rips a hole in the fabric of a family's emotional and spiritual life. It foments lies, deceit, and self-serving behavior and moves family life from a relational domain into the judicial. Divorce warps the circle of life in ways that can never be repaired. Both adults and children will carry its marks throughout life and into future generations. The theological question is not whether divorce is good, or whether divorced people are moral. Instead, it is whether families created by remarriage after divorce can be vehicles of grace and redemption for children, adults, and extended families.

Assumptions two and three assume answers to this question from the human sciences. They discourage us from reaching for redemptive visions of stepfamily life. Remarried people, they claim, cannot provide what children need. Research, our most precious purveyor of truth, shows us multiple problems that lead cultural authorities to question whether divorced and remarried families have any substantial redemptive quality. However, research is a very narrow lens. It cannot account for complex relational variables. It cannot sort out whether problems children have in stepfamilies are a result of biological parents' ongoing conflict or a function of stepfamily life. Neither can research tell us whether children raised in successful stepfamilies are any better or worse off than those raised in nuclear families.

A different kind of experienced truth is overlooked: Stepfamilies who find adequate support can succeed and produce effective children. This is probable for those who survive the first turbulent years of remarried life.

The evolutionary argument against stepfamilies is the most limiting and theologically troubling. It suggests that in human history, redemption is not likely to be embodied outside of biological ties. Human persons, men in particular, are not motivated to care for, love, or make sacrifices for someone who can give them no genetic advantage. This may explain survival of the species, but as a theological vision for human life, it falls short. It cannot envision God's impartial love embodied in human persons and expressed outside of a biological imperative. Human persons (men in particular) cannot transcend self-interest enough to express God's radically inclusive love by impartially loving stepchildren. And this is a problem if it extends to suggest that the Christian community cannot model or nurture inclusive love well enough to help stepfamilies find a welcoming, cohesive identity in step-relation love. This is, after all, the heart of the gospel of Jesus.

Our core Christian story testifies that God's love is embodied in the least likely families and in the most troubled contexts. The first chapter of Luke's gospel tells us about Mary, who found favor with God in hopeless times. This relationship led her, probably naively, into accepting an invitation to bear and raise a child in a culturally disadvantaged, nontraditional Jewish family. God risked revealing the Christ through a stepfamily. God trusted the upbringing, nurture, and care of salvation's future to Joseph, a man who would gain no biological or genetic advantage because of guaranteed parentage. Joseph's faithfulness to God's call assured care to a child that was not his. Gospel stories give us glimpses of God's love shown to Jesus through Joseph. A stepfather joined with his wife to welcome with joy a child that was not his (Luke 2). When the child was threatened by Herod's evil, Joseph left his home and livelihood to protect his stepson by fleeing to Egypt (Matthew 2). Later we see that Jesus' first twelve years in a stepfather home produced a religious knowledge and spiritual sensitivity that amazed the temple scholars (Luke 2:46). Jesus lived in a family environment that encouraged his growth, strength, and wisdom (Luke 2:39–40). When he failed to appear with the group of travelers returning to Nazareth from Jerusalem, his stepfather shared the burden of worry about his well-being.

Perhaps the most important consideration is that Jesus' family was not a "closet" stepfamily. They did not pretend to be something they weren't. It was no secret to the gospel writers that Joseph was not Jesus' father. Neither was it hidden from Jesus' contemporaries. When he taught in his hometown synagogue (Mark 6:1–5), hostile hosts called him inadequate to reveal God's love or purposes. He was not a scholar; he was a carpenter. Furthermore, his family was suspect. The most demeaning accusation was that he was a stepchild. Jesus is described in Mark 6:3 as "the son of Mary." This was not a comment about virgin birth but a typical and studied idiomatic insult. It marked Jesus as illegitimate and a stepchild who had no true standing in the community of families.[11] He was not Joseph's natural child and had no true place in the community.

The life and ministry of Jesus of Nazareth, the fullness of God's revelation, was nurtured in a countercultural, nontraditional stepfamily. From the information we have, this stepfamily provided all that was needed for him to grow in strength and wisdom and step into the mission of God's anointed. It is through a marginalized, unconventional family that God

> "…has shown strength with his arm;
>   he has scattered the proud in the thoughts of their hearts.
> He has brought down the powerful from their thrones, and lifted
>   up the lowly."
>
> (Luke 1:51–52)

Through God's impartial love, like that which Jesus experienced in his stepfamily, captives are freed and the acceptable year of the Lord is proclaimed.

Psychologists of religion remind us that core religious images are formed by experiences in early childhood. Jesus was raised in a stepfather family and emerged into adulthood with father images that expanded notions of God's love. The "Father God" that Jesus revealed loves as his own those who would be left out and fatherless. He himself was a person of suspicious family character, and he modeled God's radically inclusive love in his relationships with other suspicious folk. He ate with the outcasts, touched the lepers, and taught clearly that love in the kingdom of God transcends biological and genetic boundaries (Matthew 12:47–50). Kingdom love, Jesus taught, extends equally to those outside of kinship ties. Jesus' subversive message that cultural "stepchildren" receive an equal inheritance in the new, inbreaking kingdom of God shook the Jewish religious status quo to its foundations. It was an intolerable message then, and it is a difficult message today.

The community of faith is called to break away from nuclear family idolatry that envisions purest love attached only to biology and that assumes that worthy parents and accurate symbols of God's relationship to

---

[11]William Lane, *Commentary on the Gospel of Mark* (Grand Rapids, Mich.: Wm. B. Eerdmans Publishing Company, 1974), 202–3.

humanity are found exclusively (or most clearly) in this family form. Love informed by Jesus' gospel example must not retreat from stepchildren, stepparents, or stepfamilies. The Christian community must not assume that lesser love is lived through these families. Rather, it must interpret with these families how stepfamilies can model a kind of love that is possible *only* where love has no particular personal advantage. Stepfamily love can, and does, express one dimension of God's fullness embodied in human life. It is unfortunate that at the turn of the millennium the clearest public voice about stepfamily love comes in the form of a hit country and western song[12] rather than from any voice offered by the church.

The community of faith must empower stepfamilies to live into God's economy of impartial, inclusive love even when biology does not demand it. This contradicts voices such as Don Browning and colleagues who assert that the nuclear family must be given a prima facie value priority in all cultural, ethical, and educational values.[13] These claims are founded largely on assumptions that an ethic of equal regard, or impartiality, exists primarily in, or at least in close relation to, kin altruism. Since we are faulty human beings and fallible, the most consistent good we can hope for grows from our biology. Kin altruism, in its evolutionary demand that we care for our offspring, is the source of hope for the human family. Hence, a moral vision emerges that instructs us to value nuclear families above all others and guard them, even if it is at the public and private expense of other marginalized families. Our hope is biology, and excellence is biology informed by the Christian message. This vision is now coalescing in our emerging political, religious, social, and academic dialogue. However, models of God's love, particularly as shown in the gospel of Christ, subvert this wisdom and assert that kin altruism is not the foundation of God's economy. Neither is it an acceptable guiding ethic for family life in the Christian community. It must not be the moral imperative that judges a family because it is formed with incomplete biological ties or the standard that rejects all but nuclear families as inadequate and nonredemptive.

An alternative argument can be made from a similar foundation of human fault and fallibility. Since we are faulty and fallible, an adequate moral vision must make room for redemption of what has been lost. It must provide a foundation for ethical behavior that does not punish or further marginalize those in need of God's inclusive love. Such a vision rests in assuming that it is God's nature to restore what is broken. It is redeemed wreckage that most clearly reveals God's regenerating love.

---

[12]Brad Paisley, "He Didn't Have to Be," *Who Needs Pictures*, BMG/Arista, 1999.
[13]Browning et al., *Culture Wars*, 70.

Love, supported by God's grace, calls broken persons to a vocation of restoration. This includes a call to transcend biological boundaries. By responding to God and embodying an exile's vocational call to rebuild a home from the ashes of a former life, nonnuclear and culturally problematic families can and do provide a context for grace, hope, and love. Kin altruism is not required to do the "hard stuff" of love. Instead, it is God's inclusive love that casts out fear and destabilizes self-interest. In God's economy, a stepfather can risk giving affection freely and a stepmother can set appropriate boundaries in an atmosphere of love. Guided by Jesus' model of full acceptance of marginal people, stepchildren receive grace-full welcome into stepfamily homes from parents with whom they do not share genes. At this confluence of love and grace boils a hope of redemption rooted in God's love for folk who have lost the promise of nuclear-family success.

A redemptive vision for stepfamilies claims that divorced and remarried families can embody God's impartial love. This transcends genetic biases. This vision does not deny the sin of divorce and human failure, but relies on God's forgiveness. It recognizes the tragic loss of home in divorce and trusts God's compassionate love to guide restoration. By calling out the best of fallible humanity, it empowers stepfamilies to embody God's love and live in accountability to God's redemptive action. This vision finds its ground in the creative, redemptive, and subversive gospel, which turns dominant, culturally acceptable narratives upside down and rethinks old predispositions and commitments. Stepfamilies are not simply accidents or problems for a church or community of faith; they are central[14] foci of God's action in the community of faith. Such a call for restoration has deep implications for the church's mission. It requires that the Christian community take its gaze away from idolatries and creatively interpret the love of God in new, sometimes hard, circumstances. It demands that the church think theologically and ask hard questions about life together in the body of Christ and what inclusive love means.

Stepfamilies can and do communicate God's grace. They require the same serious theological consideration and community reflection as any other central religious vocation or relationship. The church must find ways to interpret remarriage as a redemptive vocation that demands a full sense of call and commitment. It is remarried couples' commitment and action that finds release from exile. However, remarriage is not just about adults recovering from divorce. It is also about wounded children. A call to remarriage vocation is, at its heart, an imperative toward stepparenting. The two

---

[14]A creative tension for congregations' ministering will be a continuous concern for balancing affirmation of non-divorced families with inclusion and affirmation of remarried families.

cannot be separated. In God's economy, to remarry is to embody impartial love that transcends genetic self-interest and risks the anxiety of full, equal love for both stepchildren and biological children. This vocation of hope is possible only through God's grace infused in stepfamilies through supportive Christian community.

Living this moral vision requires mutual empowerment. It is not enough for congregations to empower stepfamilies. Stepfamilies must also empower the faith community to develop liturgy and ritual inclusive of their reality. Together, they must celebrate this in worship, fellowship, and growth in the body of Christ.

PART THREE
Finding Our
Way Home

Chapter 8

Pastoral Care in Motion:
An Experimental Model for Walking
Softly in the Wilderness

Sunday morning, and I am eating breakfast alone in a bakery. What does it mean that I feel a sense of relief as I identify with an obvious pagan walking into this place at 10:30 on a Sunday morning? I look around at the young parents feeding their clean, combed children, obviously on their way to worship. Dear God, I'm so angry. I look at them and I feel judgment and disapproval.

Suddenly, I am vividly aware of my own family and my own life. I feel no similarity, no contact with these aliens. My kids are wounded, sometimes bleeding, and dressed in emotional rags tattered by my past. Instead of Oshkosh, I buy therapy in hope of a future I find impossible to grasp. This is my children's reality, and it seems out of joint with this universe I see unfolding in front of me.

Who are these phantoms around me who provide clean, unweathered homes for designer children and who, in minutes, will fill the smiling pews down the street? Maybe that's it. I resent their ability to hold themselves aloof from divorce, stepparenting, and the constant conflicts from ex-spouses, ex-grandparents, ex-friends, and kids caught in the middle. Maybe I resent their ability to believe the tarnished promise that "all is well" if you will just step into the shadow of that stained-glass cross. I feel like hiding.

Talk to me about God after you've lost your marriage; after you've seen your children's blood on your hands because of the spirit-killing traumas of divorce, single-parenting, and remarriage. Talk to me when I see the scars on your heart from enduring the pain of loss and knowing that every time your child says, "I love you daddy," she is straining at the ambivalence of betraying her mother.

Tell me, where is God in a Sunday school that forgets about my children or in worship that teaches about grace for murderers, but has no word of hope for my family? What is baptism to me? What is the eucharist to my children? Is there any blood left in the dirt at the foot of the cross for my family?[1]

A Reminder

In its most basic form, pastoral care incarnates God's loving initiative toward humans in the diversity of their life circumstances. God met Abraham in Ur, Moses in the desert, and Saul on the road to Damascus. It is God's habit to meet people where they live and intervene in the circumstances of their lives. Pastoral carers, as an embodiment of God's initiative, meet people at the point of need in specific locations. Traditionally, pastoral care has been guided by a metaphor of a shepherd who moves away from the comfort of the familiar and into the unknown to respond to another's distress without guarantee of certain outcome. This is done with sincere devotion to the other's well-being and a commitment to true engagement whether the person is on a throne or in a ditch. The shepherd responds to immediate, temporal suffering through the four pastoral functions of healing, sustaining, guiding, and reconciling while remaining rooted in the basic religious convictions of a community of faith.[2] Good pastoral care maintains the gospel tension between earth-bound response to suffering people and the ultimate concerns of the believing community among which they reside.

Care for stepfamilies must be attached to particular social locations and related to the embodied and troubling experience of their everyday social, political, economic, and emotional lives. This must be grounded firmly in a process of theological meaning-making for stepfamilies in community. Praxis, in its action-reflection motion, engages stepfamilies for one unifying purpose—to interpret the gospel of Christ in ways that include stepfamilies and empower them to share in God's promise of health, sustenance, guidance, and reconciliation. Stepfamilies need shepherds who will leave the safety of the familiar and meet them in their peculiar circumstances.

---

[1] A family counseling client's journal entry, quoted with permission and without name.
[2] Seward Hiltner, *Preface to Pastoral Theology* (Nashville: Abingdon Press, 1958).

Effective care is not about gathering professional advice to cure stepfamilies of their stress, recapitulating grief, or complex circumstances. Instead, it is an incarnational, relational encounter that leads stepfamilies to full communion with the body of Christ. It participates in changing those structures, beliefs, and processes by which they are oppressed.

Hermeneutical circularity provides a conceptual tool to guide the inclusive, critical dialogue needed for an embodied, relational encounter. It begins when stepfamily stories, with all their fears, tears, and hopes intrude on familiar community tapestries. Most stepfamilies are noticed because of their distress. When the blood of their struggle begins to stain the peripheries of church life, they gain attention. Sometimes a sudden flare of embodied pain burns too close to cherished church patterns, and a stepfamily is center stage in congregational life. Caring Christian communities notice this and are jarred. They become attentive to suppressed stories that have not been told, experiences that have not been named, and families in need of an incarnation of God's loving initiative. Less caring communities find obvious or subtle ways to reject or ignore stepfamily problems and return to safe, familiar territory.

Truly sensitive communities will notice stepfamily differences and value the diversity they bring. They will not wait for pain to drive the creative meaning-making process. Instead, they will attend to stepfamily stories in their wholeness and ask how stepfamilies embody hope in the crucible of intense loss. They will ask what stepfamily struggle means for the body of Christ and explore how they love in spite of all biological and emotional odds. Responsive congregations will listen to stepfamily voices and mutually weave them into the worshiping community's life through ongoing critical dialogue.

Whether from hearing cries of pain or from commitment to welcoming stepfamilies in their wholeness, a congregation's attitude of creative theological imagining invites stepfamilies into critical dialogue with a worshiping community. This drives the action-reflection motion of the hermeneutical process. As conversation deepens, we turn to our theological sources with new questions (see fig. 1, chap. 3). Stepfamily stories begin to affect the fabric of theological meaning-making as the gospel of Christ is interpreted anew. Together, new meanings are created, new metaphors are discovered, and caring action—healing, guiding, sustaining, and reconciling—is fermented with mutual benefit for all in the body of Christ. Stepfamilies' unique identity emerges within the body of Christ as remarried folk find empowering connections with the community. As full conversational partners, they both embody God's inclusive healing and expand the church and its theology by modeling otherwise unknown dimensions of God. Creative theological imagining creates a redemptive vision for stepfamilies that is integrated into the larger narrative of God's inclusive love and salvation. New meanings are then cultivated back into the community through its worship, teaching, care, and social relationships. In this process, stepfamily stories are no longer a problem peripheral to the church, but are integrated threads of its diverse, central story.

ORIENTING TO THE LANDSCAPE

Most families (but especially those with clear religious commitments and church affiliations) live through transitional events and celebrations in close proximity to a congregation. Many stepfamily-specific crises hide just below the surface of these rituals. When a stepfamily's emotional processes converge with weddings, funerals, baptisms, and confirmations, church members and leaders will be close to, and sometimes a part of, behavioral and affective fallout. Polls continue to show that people in trouble will turn to their pastor for help before consulting any other professional. Church leaders and pastors are likely to be first on the scene of developmental and situation crises central to stepfamily life.

Crisis-centered occasions are obvious places for congregations and pastoral carers to meet stepfamilies. Through a revolving motion of critical dialogue and care, congregations can move through the five episodes of praxis, hermeneutical circularity, and creative theological imagining.

Episode I: Initiative and Invitation

In chapter 1, we met Carol Smith, pastor of a growing suburban church, who was unceremoniously immersed in stepfamily pain in a most ungracious way. Her experience, however, pressed her to be more watchful of those families she knew to have a history of divorce and remarriage. Her story continues:

ATTENTION AND INTENTION

Two years after her episode with the Browns, Pastor Smith noticed that a new choir member, Sharon Willis, seemed despondent and appeared to be losing weight. Over two months, Sharon was ill twice and cried several times after services. When the choir director asked if she was all right, Sharon replied, "I have a lot on my mind right now."

Pastor Smith knew little about Sharon except that she attended faithfully with her husband, Larry. The family had four children, fifteen-year-old Bryan, twelve-year-old Drew, ten-year-old Mary, and eight-year-old Jon. Since the family was listed in all church correspondence as "Willis," it was only by accident that Pastor Smith knew Sharon was a stepmother. She had assumed nuclear-family relationships until Drew made a comment in a youth meeting about his mother. Clearly he was not speaking of Sharon. Remembering her episode with the Browns, Pastor Smith was careful about the fact that another stepfamily might need help in ways that were unfamiliar to her and her congregation.

Through her reading, Pastor Smith had learned that one symptom-carrying person often provides a barometer for how a stepfamily is faring. She began to wonder what care Sharon and her family might need. Since the pastoral team had noticed no particular crisis in the Willis family, Pastor Smith took the initiative to get to know Sharon a little better.

Pastor Smith's parishioners knew that her ministry style was to establish a warm, available presence with her congregation. She was fortunate to be pastor of a church with two staff members. These colleagues managed administrative details and the church's education program. She was free to engage the congregation more personally and to concentrate on preaching. Though Sharon was only one of the 250 members of her church, she would not think it unusual if Pastor Smith called and wanted to schedule time for coffee. So when the pastor called, Sharon agreed to meet that afternoon after work. Pastor Smith's agenda was to get to know Sharon a little better by inviting her to tell her story. Though she was concerned about Sharon's tears and apparent fatigue, she was determined to meet Sharon where she was and listen well.

By the end of an hour, Pastor Smith felt she had begun to befriend Sharon. She listened empathically as Sharon shared some "safe" personal history. She knew where Sharon had grown up, how she met Larry, and that the couple had been married less than a year. It seemed to Pastor Smith that Sharon's account of being a stepmother was a little "glossy." Her facial expressions didn't match the good words about her marriage, children, and stepchildren. During the conversation, Sharon smiled as she admitted things were sometimes hard in remarriage. She sighed deeply and looked "lost" when she talked about how well the four children got along. Pastor Smith also noticed that Sharon shared no success stories about children in school, sports, or scouts. Where were the stories of a proud mother she was so used to hearing from other families?

Pastor Smith discovered that the Willises had joined the church at Sharon's request. Religious life had always been important to her, but less so for Larry. She felt comfortable in this congregation. It was a traditional church that reminded her of home. It was also large enough that she could find a place without the congregation's knowing the details of her divorce and remarriage. Sharon was embarrassed by her past marital failure and was afraid she might not find genuine acceptance if people knew she and Larry were both divorced. Pastor Smith left with an agreement that she and Sharon would meet again two weeks later.

Following her visit, Pastor Smith consulted with her colleagues. She learned that Sunday school teachers had been concerned about ten-year-old Mary since her first Sunday at church four months earlier. She rarely participated in groups and seemed sad. Fifteen-year-old Bryan attended some youth meetings. He was often irritable, and youth leaders suspected a substance-abuse problem. Bryan usually showed up for a few minutes, left the church grounds, and then returned just before the meeting adjourned. Other youth who attended his school told stories about his skipping school, smoking, and being a poor student. Youth leaders were irritated with his effect on others in the group. Twelve-year-old Drew attended Sunday school and some youth meetings but did not participate much. Larry attended church on Sunday morning but was not attached to any particular congregational activity or group.

Over the next month, Pastor Smith met with Sharon twice. Each conversation exposed more of her life within her family. Pastor Smith learned that Sharon often did not know how to respond to Larry's children. She sometimes worried about how their marriage would grow if she couldn't learn to be a "good mom" to them. She tried but often felt her efforts were worth little. Without disclosing details, she shared that she was worried about both Bryan and Jon. Neither was doing well in school. She was frustrated that teachers, counselors, and principals seemed to have little help to offer a mother who was sincerely trying to motivate her children. She was angry about the principal's telling her that teachers were not expected to go out of their way to help her check on Bryan, that there were too many kids, and high school kids shouldn't need a "babysitter." She was also "a little frustrated" about church. Though she badly wanted her children involved in religious life, she felt church members stayed away from her and her family. Few people knew they were a stepfamily, but Bryan's behavior kept parents from wanting him around their children. He was a bad influence. Instead of Bryan's being positively influenced by church families, he was isolated and alienated. She understood their desire to protect their own children, but couldn't help but resent lack of support for her teenage son from his church relationships. "There's more," said Sharon, "but I can't tell you that now. Church life hasn't always been good for us."

A few weeks later, Pastor Smith was invited more fully into the Willises' home by a Saturday emergency call. Bryan had come home drunk, and Larry insisted that he leave. Sharon had taken Bryan to her brother's house in a neighboring town. On the way home, she decided she could no longer live with Larry. When she told him she was leaving, the couple talked and agreed they would take no action until she had talked to their pastor. Pastor Smith listened and suggested that she meet with both Larry and Sharon later that day.

Larry and Sharon were angry and afraid when they met Pastor Smith in her office. Within a few minutes, it was clear that the couple was in serious crisis. Both Larry and Sharon felt overwhelmed and could not talk about their experience without excessive guilt or blame for each other. Midway through the session, Pastor Smith began to plan how she would refer this couple to a pastoral counselor who had experience working with remarried couples. Her agenda now became crisis management. By the end of the session, the couple agreed to a referral for pastoral counseling. They also made plans with the pastor about how they would live together over the intervening week and do no further damage to their wounded relationship. The couple agreed for Pastor Smith to call the next day and visit them the following week.

EVALUATION

Praxis means paying attention to people in their concrete social location, noticing human predicaments, and then initiating action in the community balanced with active reflection. By reflecting critically on her experience with the Browns, Pastor Smith changed her approach to stepfamilies in her congregation. She was no longer willing to assume that experience in a first-married nuclear family or her seminary education about families was an adequate guide for congregational care. Neither was she willing to trust that remarried couples would be easily forthcoming about their lives.

Reading about stepfamilies helped her attend more clearly to behavior when Sharon showed signs of fatigue and pain. However, her reading provided little clear information about how to respond. Carefully, from an inexpert position of not knowing, Pastor Smith initiated contact with Sharon first by treating her as a true member of the community of faith. By inviting her into conversation, Pastor Smith let Sharon know that her voice was valued and her story worth hearing. From the position of a compassionate listener and conversational partner, Pastor Smith avoided expert assumptions about what stepfamilies or stepmothers should be, think, or feel. Instead, she allowed Sharon to instruct her about the truths and vicissitudes of her own and her family's life.

Pastor Smith's intent had been to invite the Willis family more completely into the life and care of the church. When she approached Sharon, she had no formal plan for how this should happen. Through sharing stories, she believed, relational connections and mutual meanings would emerge that would become part of the fabric of the broader community of faith.

Eventually, the Willis family story would become an integral part of the church's story. She hoped her initiative with Sharon would establish a connection and provide a pastoral gate into full community life. This would be a safe, nonthreatening holding space that could provide stabilizing support for the family. If crises did erupt, this community foundation would be a solid foundation for care the family might need.

However, Willis family dynamics had a life of their own and arced across the poles of Pastor Smith's carefully considered pastoral plan. She quickly found herself immersed in a stepfamily crisis that drove her to new levels of action and reflection. Her first step after the couple's emergency call was to affirm her relationship with Sharon. She responded immediately and attended to what she had learned in shared conversations. She knew that Sharon valued her marriage, was afraid to fail, was sad about what her children had endured, and worked hard to control anger in a situation she sometimes felt was impossible. When she requested that both Sharon and Larry come for a joint conversation with her, she supported Sharon's marital values and integrated her own hope for the couple and for the family's success.

In the session itself, Pastor Smith continued to make reflective decisions based on her pastoral value system and her growing interaction with the couple. Though it was tempting to refer the couple to a therapist and withdraw from their incendiary story, she took time in the session to consider the couple in their relational context. She concluded that a referral only would remove Larry and Sharon from other sources of congregational support. She decided to become more, not less, engaged with the couple and their conflict. This took two forms. First, she carefully balanced her conversation in the session so that both Larry and Sharon felt heard and valued. Second, she made a referral to a pastoral therapist in language that assumed that the Willises would continue to be in contact with her and the church. Her orientation to this future expressed hope for the couple and an incarnational promise that they would not be abandoned by the community they were just beginning to know. She hoped this would provide stabilizing resources while they waited for therapeutic help as well as invite them to turn toward, rather than away from, a community of support.

Pastor Smith's action placed her and her congregation on a shaky limb. Jarred by the Willises' experience, she took initiative to promise community support in a tense stepfamily situation. This would force her and the community of faith to reflect more deeply on how the congregation and pastoral leadership should respond to family crises, and more specifically, to very complicated stepfamily crises.

Episode II: Engagement

Pastor Smith considered the Willises. The family was within what she knew to be the dangerous first two years of stepfamily life. She also knew that since both had custody of their children, they were living in the most difficult of circumstances. From her conversations, she also suspected that Larry and Sharon had unrealistic expectations of stepfamily life, which is characteristic of romantic remarried couples. Because Bryan was entering adolescence, she was not surprised that he was the fulcrum of family pain. Furthermore, the entire family seemed isolated from congregational and other community support. At church, they were present but rarely engaged. Other new families took time getting to know people, but the Willises seemed to have no connection apart from Sharon's willingness to talk with Pastor Smith.

Pastor Smith began to consider a plan of care. She had made well-meaning promises to the Willises about the church's caring support. These were based in her belief that God's redeeming love is embodied in Christian community. However, without intentional reflection and action by the congregation, promises implied were likely to be meaningless to Larry and Sharon.

Pastor Smith's first step was to consult her colleagues and discuss what kinds of ministries might be helpful to stepfamilies. Initially the staff wondered how large a "problem" stepfamilies were. One colleague admitted embarrassment. Besides the Willises, he could name only one other stepfamily in the congregation. Statistically, he knew there had to be more. Why were they so invisible, and what could the church do? The team considered specialized stepfamily support groups led by a family therapist and educational events to sensitize the congregation to stepfamily needs. By meeting's end, the staff decided they needed more information about what other churches found successful with stepfamilies. Several telephone calls later, they found that many churches had concerns about stepfamilies. Few had any experience with specialized stepfamily ministries. Several congregations had hosted educational events. These were usually poorly attended except by grandparents of children who lived in stepfamilies. One church sponsored stepfamily support groups that were peripheral to the church's main activities. The pastor was not certain how effective these were or how many people attended.

Pastor Smith and her colleagues concluded they would have to risk unknown territory if they were to expand with integrity pastoral care to stepfamilies. They first reviewed foundations for their ministry. They believed in collaborative, empowering leadership that invites congregation members to assume responsibility for interpreting their situation and making decisions about their own future.[3] Empowering leadership includes the stranger—such as a stepfamily—as a full partner in the interpretive conversation. Stepfamily strangers are not foreign influences that bear threatening values. Neither are they needy consumers of congregational resources. Rather, they are bearers of wisdom and insight who expand and broaden our understanding of God and the gospel. Collaborative leadership, concluded the team, must engage the Willises and other stepfamilies to interpret their situation and its intersection with the gospel. The team's first priority was to find a way to join with stepfamilies to talk about family life in the community of faith. This reflection could inform new action in the congregation, which would then fuel further reflection and a renewed interpretation of the gospel.

Both Pastor Smith and her colleagues agreed that the challenge for ministry was not only stepfamilies. The Willis family had jarred their sensibilities and presented an immediate crisis that pointed to one kind of family that needed attention. The larger question was how the church responds to a "stranger." Stepfamilies were not unknown, but neither were they comfortably familiar. The church would need to embrace diversity and some creative conflict with an "unknown other." At the same time, remarried couples, such as the Willises, would need to feel safe and welcome enough to participate.

Pastor Smith pointed out that there were few public forums in which to talk openly about family life. Most workshops and public conversations were politically motivated—to legitimize stepfamilies and single-parent families at any cost or to support nuclear family life at the cost of all others. She saw a need for empowering conversations *between* families and collaborative leaders. The church needed space and time to listen to voices that were rarely heard. The stories these voices told should be integrated into a critical conversation about families and faith. New voices and new stories would show new possibilites for God's activity in the community of Christ. Pastor Smith believed that care for marginalized families is rooted in a mutual commitment to God's inclusive love as revealed in the gospel of Christ. It is supported by compassionate connection within the community of faith, and it empowers those whose lives have been touched by tragedy and injustice. Radically inclusive love finds mutuality and risks dialogue about sensitive issues. Stepfamily strangers can then risk empowerment.

---

[3]See John McClure, *The Round-table Pulpit: Where Leadership and Preaching Meet* (Nashville: Abingdon Press, 1995).

The ministry team agreed to an experiment in praxis. Pastor Smith's contact with Sharon and Larry started in private conversation. Since praxis is a collaborative, community event, the next step would be to expand the system beyond the individual pastor and solitary family. With great thought, the ministry team constructed a list of individuals and couples to invite to a weekly group to talk about "families and the life of the church." It was described as a forum to hear family stories and talk about how they related to the gospel message. By design, it was to include both strong church supporters and those more marginal. The forum's goal was to collaborate with the ministry team and guide the empowering of ministries with families.

The team invited Larry and Sharon, a remarried couple who had a several-year history with the church (David and Louise), an older first-married couple who were church leaders (Amy and John), a middle-aged first-married couple who attended irregularly (Janice and Charles), a single parent who was a children's Sunday school teacher (Mary), and a single parent who was marginally connected to the church (Jim). The group was scheduled to meet during regular church program hours on Sunday evening. Child care and an evening meal were provided. Pastor Smith personally invited each forum member. Though marginal church members were skeptical about their invitation, each agreed.

Larry and Sharon were reluctant to participate when Pastor Smith invited them. They did not want to feel singled out because of their problems, nor did they want their pain made worse by talking about conflictual issues within a group. Pastor Smith emphasized the group's purpose and reassured the couple that they would not be asked to disclose anything they felt was unsafe. Larry and Sharon agreed to join for six weeks, comforted by the fact that another stepfamily would attend. They would not be "hanging out there alone" among people who had no contact with their experience.

The forum began as Pastor Smith set some informal ground rules. First, this was not a therapy group. Their mission was to listen for the variety of family stories imbedded in the group members' experience. The object was not to offer help but to hear others' experience clearly. They would pay attention to common and uncommon themes in the stories that were shared. Together, they would help each voice the meanings contained in the stories families lived. As the group developed, they would consider what various narrative themes meant to their life together in Christ. Pastor Smith began the first session by asking, "What is it like to be your family in today's world?"

Larry and Sharon silently listened to more outspoken couples tell their family stories. In the third session, Sharon and Larry began to share. They felt empowered by other couples' struggles to talk about their own experience.

As they learned to trust the group, they disclosed more about how difficult it was to live with children who are not your own and how trying it was to set rules in a household that was always arguing about who was in charge. In the fifth meeting, Janice, a traditional nuclear-family mother commented, "I just can't imagine what it must have been like to go through a divorce and then try to make a family again. I can only imagine that sometimes it feels like hell. I love you and Larry. You two make a good couple, but I'm so sorry you had to lose so much to get what you have."

This comment stunned Sharon. Through her tears, she told her story of divorce and how much it hurt. Because of that event, she felt life would never be right. Her family was permanently and unalterably changed. Her children were in trouble, and she was an outcast. In the next session, Sharon and Larry told important parts of their stepfamily story. They were able to talk about their losses in divorce, how their expectations of a new marriage were violated, and how helpless they felt as parents to their children and stepchildren. Janice's empathic response had solidified the group as a safe place to share.

As Larry and Sharon disclosed increasingly raw parts of their story, the forum listened and asked questions about their experience. Divorced members of the group affirmed them and shared parts of their own stories. David and Louise, who had been divorced and remarried years before, recalled some of their early remarriage stories. These reassured Sharon and Larry as they compared the older couple's experience with their own. Several times, forum members offered advice to those who shared. Pastor Smith gently reminded the group of its purpose. This was not therapy. They were not to try to "fix" others' problems. They were to listen in order to understand another's experience.

By the end of the eight-week contract, a variety of family stories had emerged. The group could talk about how different nuclear-family stories were from the stories of those who had been divorced. Stepfamily and single-parent stories bloomed with a variety of colors and textures. Because Larry and Sharon's story was permeated with palpable distress, it was a central focus of the forum. What had begun as a jarring event in Pastor Smith's ministry was now a part of the community's story. Forum members engaged Sharon and Larry, heard their story, and were jarred. With Pastor Smith's help they began to move through a hermeneutical cycle.

EVALUATION

A safe place to tell the truth. Once a pastoral encounter jars a community into awareness, the hermeneutical cycle of creative theological imagining[4] presses praxis for more information. The active-reflective community must find ways to elicit, hear, and engage the stories that give meaning to jarring experience and demand response. Sharing stories is a risky business for both the teller and the community that receives them. On one hand, people who honestly share risk misunderstanding, judgment, rejection, and further marginalization. On the other hand, communities that lock eyes with the storyteller and receive the effects of embodied experience risk engagement that compels them further into the hermeneutical cycle. There they will be forced to examine their assumptions, perceptions, and actions in the light of new stories that break old molds. Well-known ways of being a congregation are challenged when God's love includes new, "foreign" people and their stories. If otherness is taken seriously, it always calls us to new facts and values that will potentially transform life.

Pastor Smith's first contact with Larry and Sharon was quiet and private. She noticed Sharon's early distress and initiated an individual response. In the confidentiality of pastoral conversation, Sharon tested whether she could be honest and safe at the same time. She was not disappointed. When crisis erupted, her confidence in Pastor Smith's compassion allowed her to tell the truth about her relationship with Larry and her stepfamily. It would have been easy for Pastor Smith to protect the community from Larry and Sharon's truth by keeping conversations private and turning the couple over to a family therapist. Instead, she trusted her perception that "stepfamily strangers" did not have full access to the restoring gospel embodied in the community of faith. This concerned her. She knew that how she diagnosed the problem would determine its treatment. If she assumed pathology in Larry, Sharon, or their children, she could justify referring them for a "cure." However, if she saw their problem as connected to the church's struggle to avoid differentness and stepfamily pain, pastoral intervention would take another course. She would have to be a catalyst that encouraged engagement between the Willis family and a congregation struggling to embody God's inclusive love. This guided her next steps.

By consulting with the ministry team, Pastor Smith moved the jarring experience out of the private realm and onto the edge of community life. Collaborative reflection led by the team organized a way to engage the Willises and expand congregational frames of reference. By inviting stepfamilies to share their stories, they hoped to provide an active-reflective forum for stepfamily empowerment. The team intended to expand critical conversation and explore how God's love finds expression with and through stepfamily strangers. Pastor Smith and her colleagues knew that such conversations are meant to transform communities. Privatizing

---

[4]See chapter 3, figure 1.

commitments, such as group confidentiality, were specifically avoided. Instead, Pastor Smith focused on safety in the community of faith and called group members to empowered choice about what they would or would not disclose. To insist on confidentiality would have undermined the active-reflective purpose of a community struggling with inclusion and otherness.

Subjugated, marginalized voices are heard when compassion supports safety, respect, and a non-pressured space for silence and the tentative story of the strange "other." They are also heard when the burden of invisibility, voicelessness, and injustice presses marginalized people into defiance. Defiance tells subjugated stories in strident screams of rage without regard for safety or the continued integrity of the community. The Christian community is a metaphor of compassionate safety. We attend, engage, and befriend. We hope, as Nelle Morton suggests, to "hear people into speech."[5] Hearing stepfamilies into speech means refusing to coerce them into the stories we want or rushing to fill silences with our own fearful speech. It means being aware of the other, attending to the other, and empathically entering their world with a promise to value their truth faithfully. An active-reflective ministry of engagement means creating a safe place where the truth can be told and heard, where new information can be integrated into the whole of the congregation, and where the community can be challenged to scream in defiance with marginalized people when that is an obvious act of love and solidarity.

Sharon and Larry's tentative voices emerged through the forum. They were not coerced. Neither was their silence filled with anxious pronouncements about stepfamily life by pastors or other well-meaning forum members. When Sharon risked disclosing her lived truth, she was met with empathy and compassion. As she and Larry found safety, they risked more of their truth and became bearers of a valuable story. They were no longer just troubled people who were a drain on congregational resources. They were contributors to congregational life. Engagement where it was safe to tell the truth projected the forum and congregation into the next episode of praxis, hermeneutical circularity, and creative theological imagining.

Episode III: Expanded Stories and Critical Conversation

At the end of eight sessions, all forum members agreed to continue for another twelve weeks. Their agenda would be "family stories," but now they would consider how their stories connected with narratives of faith and congregational life. Pastor Smith again initiated the conversation with

---

[5]Nelle Morton, *The Journey is Home* (Boston: Beacon Press, 1985), 55–56.

a question: "How has the church and religious teaching helped or influenced your family life?"

Amy and John, an older couple who had raised children in a nuclear family, quickly responded. They had grown up in church, met in church, and raised their children in church. Religious teaching and congregational life had supported them well through years of marriage. Though their problems were different from Larry and Sharon's, John remembered painful marital problems and difficulties with adolescent children. Marriage enrichment, youth groups, and caring leaders had helped them through crises. Worship also helped. They found comfort in biblical passages and sermons promising God's presence in hard times. Amy remembered sermons and Sunday school classes that helped her be a better parent. Janice and Charles, another first-married couple in the forum, agreed. Religious life had also been good for them. In fact, they had started attending church only after their first child was born. It was important that their children have spiritual guidance. They continued to encourage their teenagers to participate in youth activities. Though they could not point to specific sermons, doctrines, or biblical images, church relationships had nourished them.

Mary, a single parent in the group, remarked that her feelings about the church and its teachings changed after her divorce. She told how difficult it had been for her to tell her friends and minister that she and her husband were separating. The pastor visited the couple's home and set up appointments to "save the marriage." These had not gone well, and Mary withdrew from congregational life. In nearly a year, no one from the church visited or called. When she returned, people were happy to see her but did not know what to say. She never talked with anyone from the church about her divorce or how she was feeling. She felt alone in congregational life even though she attended church-sponsored divorce recovery groups. These rarely intersected with "regular" congregational life, since few group members belonged to the church.

Pastor Smith asked Mary what was missing in her relationship with the church. Slowly, Mary recalled, "This was the most traumatic event in my life. It tore my world apart. At a time when I couldn't function or see any reason to go on, prayer was barren, sermons were empty, and no one seemed to care that I couldn't go on. The only word I got was, 'Buck up, hang in there, it'll pass.' I think most people didn't want to see me at all. Others acted like I had committed the unpardonable sin by divorcing. I don't think anybody saw how deeply I was crushed or how afraid I was." Pastor Smith responded, "It sounds like you feel the whole church missed the tragedy your family lived through."

Mary's story turned the group to thinking of divorce as tragedy. This was a new idea for first-married couples. People chose to divorce. It wasn't something forced on them. Larry and Louise each pointed to their own stories. They had no choice in their divorces. To be abandoned felt hopelessly and helplessly tragic. An "evil" outside of their control took over and swept away their future. Other divorced people in the group talked about floods of loss, sin, and brokenness that could only be described as tragic. The experience was profound, even for those who had initiated their own divorces. Together they began to explore "tragedy" as a symbol of immense loss that follows a divorced-family system through years and subsequent relationships. The group's stories showed that divorce left clear footprints of suffering and sadness through every phase of human development. Pastor Smith wondered out loud, "What does our Christian tradition offer people who suffer tragedy?"

The next week the forum explored what biblical tradition, theology, and the community of Christ offered people who suffered tragedy. The group first asked whether divorced people deserved what they got. Jim proposed that divorce was sin, and it resulted in suffering. As morally free agents, we make decisions and must pay the price for our actions. The guilt he bore for his own marital failure was necessary and unavoidable. He expected to suffer because of his sin. Tragedy suggests a cosmic force in which people have limited freedom to resist or decide. This he rejected, calling it a way to avoid responsibility.

Mary and Sharon disagreed. They believed there were factors and forces beyond their control. Their freedom was not absolute. Sharon was convinced that mental disease was as much a factor in her divorce as moral choice. That was tragedy. Mary felt it was tragic when a marital partner had to choose between irreconcilable moral obligations. Should she stay in a marriage with an abusive husband to uphold the value of one-time marriage, or should she save her and her children's lives? This also was tragedy. And, continued Sharon, how can freedom or moral choice account for children's suffering? They have no choice and are victims of forces beyond their control. She believed Bryan was an example of a child overcome by tragedy who lived in chronic suffering. It was unjust that he suffered because of others' sin. This, concluded Sharon, was tragic.

Pastor Smith summarized what she heard: Divorced people suffer. They live with a shadow of loss and grief because of what has happened to them. Sin is central, and guilt is a natural corollary of sin. But there is more than guilt and suffering. There seem to be tragic forces at work that keep divorced people from full recovery. Divorce destroys its victims in ways that are not entirely deserved. Social and religious forces collude with divorce processes to isolate and alienate divorced people and their families. Pastor Smith pointed to Wendy Farley's[6] notion that human actions, such as divorce, take place in an environment that is not entirely shaped by human decisions or desire. We live in an embodied world of conflict that makes human life possible but also makes suffering inevitable. Pastor Smith suggested that divorced families are affected by both sin and tragedy. In a context of freedom and conflict, sin undermines relationships. It pierces the human spirit because of indifference to evil or a desire for evil. She pointed to Larry's, Jim's, and Mary's examples of sinful choices that precipitated marital failure. On the other hand, tragedy was present too. Individual and family spirits were crippled by forces greater than sin. This was seen in Bryan's distress, the Willises' loss of hope and future, and Mary's decreased ability to trust affection. These overstepped the boundaries of guilt related to sin.

Sin's bondage is broken through accountability. Guilt is replaced by forgiveness and atonement. However, divorce also produces a form of tragic suffering that cripples the human spirit in ways that cannot be redeemed through accountability for personal sin. Part of this is cultural. Economic and social forces beyond individual control collude to put couples in impossible situations that cannot be solved. The weight of daily life in our complex world erodes values that support marriage and breaks embattled spouses' and parents' resolve.

While individuals carry the weight of divorce with very little help, marital failure does not happen in a vacuum. It is complex and has a life of its own beyond individual decision. Its mark on divorced and remarried people is a loss of hope in promise that borders on nihilism. It is tragic and smothers the human spirit. Children carry the weight of decisions they did not make and over which they have no control. Bryan, for instance, carried the weight of his own behavior. This awaited forgiveness and reconciliation. However, his behavior was also part of a larger picture of tragic events that happened *to* him. In the stories she heard, pastor Smith believed she found both tragedy and sin.

As the conversation continued, the group found more examples of sin and tragedy in divorce stories. These were woven through the entire fabric of single-parent and stepfamily stories. Probing these provoked a deep sense of sadness and loss. Amy raised the question, "If healing from sin comes through accountability, forgiveness, and atonement, what about tragedy? How does God respond to Sharon, Mary, Larry, and their kids? Is there any hope?"

---

[6]Wendy Farley, *Tragic Vision and Divine Compassion: A Contemporary Theodicy* (Louisville: Westminster/John Knox Press, 1990).

John, who read widely in biblical and theological areas, pointed out that Jesus came to bind up the brokenhearted and to set the captives free. These were powerful images in both the Hebrew Scriptures and the New Testament. The center of Jesus' ministry, he claimed, was God meeting people in their grief in order to offer hope. Wasn't that the point of the crucifixion? Wasn't that the central symbol of the Lord's supper—hope redeemed through blood shed and a broken body? Was there any event so tragic as Jesus' death, which the supper symbolized? In his opinion, the ritual was Jesus' way of reminding the disciples and later generations that he knew what it meant to suffer and be forsaken.

When we join in Christian communion, we touch Jesus' broken body and shed blood. We are reminded that he suffered, and take part in that which was central to his incarnation. Situated in a world of sin, Jesus accepted the results of forces that work against good and against God. In giving himself to the cross, he stood in union with those who suffer tragic loss. His resurrection is hope incarnate that God truly restores that which has been lost to sin and evil. God proclaims resurrection, heals that which is irretrievably broken. Communion joins us together with that present and future hope.

Pastor Smith's interest was sparked by this conversation. She saw rich, reflective resources in the new voices and insights being expressed in the group and asked them to collaborate[7] with her on two sermons about sin, tragedy, and hope. She saw this as theologically constructive activity that would do three things. First, it would speak to divorced and remarried people who felt their experience was not valued by the community of faith. She reminded the group of their criticism: Never had they heard a constructive sermon about divorce or remarriage. Second, a collaborative preaching event would value divorced and remarried people as bearers of wisdom who could help interpret the gospel in the light of their experience. Third, by bringing the forum's praxis work to the broader congregation, voices of "familiar strangers" would begin to be integrated into the whole life of the church. Forum members agreed and continued to talk with Pastor Smith about sin, loss, tragedy, and God's response. The soil for discussion and sermon construction was divorce and remarriage stories. Those never divorced were enlisted to empower these voices by framing the discussion, identifying points of connection with first-married experience, and challenging the process by maintaining integrity with how their stories were different from divorce and remarriage narratives.

---

[7]McClure, *Round-table Pulpit*, 164.

Pastor Smith pointed out that their discussion opened several questions that demanded new answers. If divorce and remarriage are framed not just by sin, but also by tragedy, what does this mean for the community of faith? It is not enough to point out a tragic vision for divorced families without relating it to other themes central to the Christian community. For instance, how does sin and guilt or tragedy and brokenness relate to God's promise of restoration and healing? How does this apply concretely to divorced and remarried families?

For two sessions, the forum reflected on gospel themes and the psalms. From stories of abandonment in divorce, of failed community, and of wounded children, a hope emerged. God is love, and God's love is expressed through compassion for those who are wounded and suffering. It is God's compassion, embodied in the good Samaritan, Jesus' response to the outcasts, and the psalmists' poetry that offers the only hope for full restoration after divorce. God recognizes suffering and cares. John recited two scriptures that came to his mind:

> The LORD is near to the brokenhearted,
>   and saves the crushed in spirit. (Psalm 34:18)

> O afflicted one, storm-tossed, and not comforted,
> I am about to set your stones in antimony,
>   and lay your foundations with sapphires. (Isaiah 54:11)

He was convinced that God saw Bryan's tragedy. God promised to respond. "But how?" asked the group. How is God's compassion incarnate to Bryan? How is it embodied to singles who can find no community or to remarried couples who are struggling beyond all strength under the weight of tragic dynamics?

Compassion, Pastor Smith suggested, is love as it encounters suffering. Compassion enters a circumstance broken by suffering not just to suffer with those who are hurt but to redeem the broken situation. For instance, the love God expressed to the world through Jesus was broken by evil and suffering. God acted with compassion by hearing the disciples' grief and sadness and also by restoring their loss. Resurrection returned Jesus to the grieving community. God's incarnate love was restored in the body of the resurrection community. God met tragedy with both empathic understanding and redeeming defiance. This, Pastor Smith thought, is what we celebrate in communion.

One group member asked again what this meant for Bryan and others suffering with the recirculating grief of divorce tragedy and loss. It is one thing to talk about the concept; it is quite another to make a difference in a suffering teen's life. Pastor Smith replied that responding to people in need means trying to see them through God's compassionate eyes. Using Bryan as an example, she and Sharon talked about how school teachers, youth leaders, and she as a parent had seen Bryan as an obstreperous, unmanageable, self-centered teen bent on destruction. What happened when God's eyes were focused on Bryan? What was seen then? The group agreed that through God's eyes, Bryan was a youth on the verge of destruction. God cared. God's heart was broken in Bryan's behalf. God was afraid and scared for him. Bryan was not a "bad child" of a "bad seed" or a child with incompetent parents who couldn't control him. Bryan was a child who had exhausted all his resources for coping with a situation beyond his or his parents' control. He was falling apart. He was a child in need of God's compassion and love.

Jim argued that this was a wonderful frame, but it still gave no concrete direction for responding to Bryan. Bryan, Larry, Sharon, and their whole family needed concrete help. Where was it? Perhaps, responded Pastor Smith, it is our business as the body of Christ to be in *communion* with those who suffer. We need to experience their pain as they experience it and love them. This kind of love soothes a wounded spirit. It engenders comfort and empowers a sufferer to bear the pain of tragedy. It helps the sufferer to resist the humiliation of self-degrading behavior and to overcome guilt. Whatever we do in the face of tragedy, our compassion must love in a way that defies sin and evil. For Bryan, it means compassion that accurately names his suffering, stands with him, and helps him resist the powers of tragedy that are beyond his control. That is the task of the faithful, resurrection community. She asked the group to consider over the next week or two what this might look like for Bryan and the Willis family.

Pastor Smith's sermon the following week centered on God's call to respond to hurting families. Referring directly to the forum's work, she named the loss and pain in divorce. She expressed the tragic quality of failed marriage in our culture and explored with the congregation how God's love includes those who are brokenhearted and captive. Throughout her sermon, she drew from the experiences and illustrations she had developed with the forum. She closed her sermon by relating the church's ministry to wounded families in the congregation and its call to incarnate God's compassionate love. She challenged the congregation to consider with her what faithful communion with divorced and remarried people might be.

EVALUATION

In Episode III, the active-reflective motion of praxis continues. Divorced and remarried people's experiences have jarred the group. In this episode, the forum found its theological framework and resources inadequate to include hurting people whom they now knew. Reflecting on the need for transformation, the forum turned to theological sources with new questions. Gospel stories, biblical themes, and theological metaphors were brought to questions of sin, suffering, loss, and grief in divorced and remarried life. This, in turn, was related to the congregation's families who needed care. By the end of Episode III, reflection compelled the forum to test what compassionate care meant for the Willis family. Their reflection moved to action as Pastor Smith integrated it into her preaching and challenge to the congregation.

Episode IV: Action and Theological Meaning-Making

In response to Pastor Smith's sermon, twenty-year-old Leah made an appointment to talk with her. She felt moved by Pastor Smith's challenge to the congregation. Her parents had divorced when she was five, and she had grown up in a stepfamily. She had attended church regularly but was not attached to Sunday school or youth groups. Leah continued:

> Everyone just seemed different from me, I guess. I heard you ask what would be helpful to people like me. I started thinking. You know, in twelve years of divorce and stepfamily, nobody ever really, truly, asked me how I was doing. Sure, people would say "How are you today?" or "Is everything going all right?" And when I said what I was supposed to, "Yeah, everything's all right," they were satisfied. When I was twelve, I gained weight awfully. When I was sixteen, I was almost anorexic. I know people noticed, because I know they talked about me. But nobody in my church ever took the time to get to know me so they could ask what was really going on. I would have told them. All I had were my parents. I didn't think I could really be honest with them. They were scared. They would have freaked and felt guilty if I told them how I really felt. My friends kind of understood, but their answers were drugs, alcohol, or acting up. I just wish that somebody—the youth director, my Sunday school teacher, or a pastor—had really cared about what I felt.

Pastor Smith asked Leah if she would be willing to attend forum meetings and take part in conversations about divorced and remarried families. She agreed.

At its next meeting, the group welcomed Leah and continued discussing how their congregation might see hurting people in divorced families through God's compassionate love. How, wondered the group, could a church live out resistance and defiance of tragedy? Sharon shared that she struggled with this idea. She wanted to overcome tragedy in her own stepfamily, but it seemed to compound instead. In the last week, the Willises' family therapist had suggested that it might be better if Bryan did not return home. His life had stabilized with his uncle. He was no longer sneaking out at night, and his drinking was contained. Sharon was angry and hurt by the therapist's suggestion. All this talk about resistance and defiance, and now they might never be the close, harmonious family she and Larry had planned. This was not fair or just.

The forum heard Sharon's anger and desire for justice. They listened to her tears and sadness as she confronted loss and the tragedy of her son's pain. Quietly, Louise recalled "losing" her own son. As she held Sharon's hand, she talked about her own grief and loss when her son told her in high school that he wanted to live with his father. That event, said Louise, felt harder than her divorce. It was not fair after all she had invested in him. It took two years to come to terms with it. Louise wondered with Sharon if rebuilding a nuclear family was the only way to heal divorce tragedy. This seemed inconsistent with the forum's discussion. Hadn't they talked at length about how nuclear family images could be idolatry? Why did mom, dad, and all the kids in harmony at home have to be the only way they could be a successful family? Louise believed that she and David had a successful stepfamily, even though it did not include all their children every day.

Pastor Smith pointed out that the group had an opportunity to live out their faith commitments with the Willises. How could they be a faithful companion to them as they walked through another stepfamily transition loaded with more grief? Their expectations were being picked apart. Larry felt guilty about his failed relationship with Bryan. Sharon was angry with Larry and sorrowing about lost family dreams. How could the group embody God's compassionate love? The forum discussed ways to support Larry and Sharon through telephone calls, reassurance of love from the group, and a commitment to pray with them. They would continue to talk as a group about changes and how they might be redemptive. Pastor Smith reminded the group that they could not "fix" anything. There was no expert among them who knew what the "right thing" was for the Willises. Their purpose was to embody the empowering, compassionate love of God that would help Larry and Sharon act in their own best interest.

Leah interrupted the reflection process by reminding the group that Larry and Sharon's children were left out. How did Bryan feel about all of this? What about Jon, his younger brother? Or, for that matter, Drew and Mary? Telling her own story, Leah asked the forum to make sure that congregational responses to the Willises did not overlook important changes in the whole family's life. The forum asked Pastor Smith to consult with youth leaders and Sunday school teachers. Those who were comfortable with the process would make a special effort to stay close to Larry and Sharon's children so they could feel a compassionate presence and voice their own stories. Since Leah knew Bryan from youth group activities, she would visit him with Sharon over the next few weeks.

For two months Larry, Sharon, and Bryan struggled with Bryan's future in the family. Each week, Larry and Sharon shared their experiences with the group. Near the end of the second month, Sharon told the group how she had tried to look at Bryan through God's compassionate eyes. Her talks with the forum had helped her see his position much better. Even though her family expectations were now more realistic, she believed Bryan did not have the personal resources to live in a situation that brought so much pressure into his life. He was having enough difficulty with normal adolescent changes. Stepfamily changes were too much for him. She asked the group to help her find God's love and redemption.

Leah spoke at once. She could see God's redemption at work in several ways. First, Bryan was passing in school and had stopped drinking. Surely this was redemption. Furthermore, he had a mother who would consider sacrificing her own desire to have all her children living at home in order to get Bryan away from pressure that was too intense. If his absence from home wasn't redemptive for Larry and Sharon, it certainly seemed to be for Bryan. Louise interjected that God's grace was present in Sharon's brother, who had taken Bryan in when his own father would not cooperate. Was this God's love incarnate? God also seemed to be working in Larry and Sharon's lives. As the group had prayed together and talked, anxiety about their situation had diminished. Larry and Sharon did not suffer under the same burden of conflict and self-recrimination. Is this how God's love is incarnate through faithful communion in the body of Christ?

Over the next week, Sharon made arrangements for Bryan to live with his uncle indefinitely. The forum continued to question how God acts in tragedy. Sharon worked with her therapist to decide how to have regular family contact with Bryan and stay connected to him as "Mom." The group discussed these changes and helped her clarify what would feel redemptive to her in this muddle of loss. Sharon mused that this was the first time she had felt loved and cared for by any group of people. She was doing the best she knew how. These people knew it and supported her.

As Sharon brought her experience back to the group for reflection, the forum discussed new theological insights they gained by sharing her experience. They had seen a small healing of tragedy because of God's compassionate love expressed in the body of Christ. The group and Sharon's brother had loved in ways that were unusual for them. God's grace and salvation seemed to come in forms they might easily have missed. Most of all, the group explored a new understanding of communion. They had shared together in the broken body and shed blood of a family. By remembering and embodying God's presence in loss, a hope for recovery was born. By "communing with the saints," Larry, Sharon, and Bryan were empowered to make difficult decisions and knew they were loved and supported.

Redemption's form was not easy for the group to see. Like the disciples who lost Jesus, resurrection hope was overshadowed by a desperate situation. For all intents and purposes, the Willis family was suffering more fragmentation by "losing" Bryan. Yet it was in this loss that hope was found for this stepfamily's most intense problem. As they prayed and walked down their own "road to Emmaus," God was active. Bryan's progress was not yet a full "resurrection," but it was at least a small resuscitation. God's redemption was not a restored nuclear family for Larry and Sharon. Instead, it was a group of people who loved them, suffered with them, and were willing to help them look beyond the traditional to a new future.

Pastor Smith guided the forum to consider what meaning this new insight into God's love and compassion had for the entire church. How should it impact her preaching and the church's teaching ministry? Were there particular times when liturgy should reflect new ways that God works through the communion of saints to redeem tragedy? Together, the forum built another sermon. This one focused on compassion that attends to people's daily lives. It presented a theology that names pain honestly and then looks for ways that God's compassion leads to defiance and redemption. It expressed a vision of Christ embodied in a congregation who touches those reeling from tragic events, stays with them, prays with them, and empowers them to make hard decisions in hope of recovery.

Pastor Smith preached the sermon on a communion Sunday. Her invitation to the table specifically included divorced and remarried people who look to the broken body and shed blood of Christ as a symbol of God's understanding their pain. She pointed to the resurrection as their true hope for restoration and healing. In the weeks following her sermon, the ministry team explored how Sunday school teachers and other church leaders could be trained to notice pain and call the community to respond. The team also looked at how their own church administration participated, or failed to participate, in redemptive change for divorced and remarried people. They explored policies, schedules, and events that might keep divorced families from full inclusion in the life of the church.

The forum continued for another year. Through cycles of critical dialogue, the congregation's response to primary stepfamily issues was strengthened, and the ministry of the church was enhanced by empowered stepfamilies cultivating their strength and unique contributions to shared life in Christ.

Evaluation

Episode IV illustrates how embodied experience and the congregation's critical dialogue participates in an action-reflection motion that not only directs care but also expands the church's theology. As people's lives are transformed by new action, we are forced to consider renewed notions of God's creative and redemptive activity. Pastoral care becomes not a religious application of behavioral sciences but a constructive theological activity. Strangers, even "familiar strangers" such as stepfamilies, ignite the hermeneutical circle. Responsible congregations are drawn to transforming dialogue. Pastoral ministry, as Pastor Smith's action shows, guides hermeneutical circulation, helps the congregation put concrete form to praxis, and articulates new theological meaning in a public language of discourse.

Episode V: The Church as Public Forum

As the forum continued to meet, the church lived with new insights that found their way into congregational life. Not all of these were positive. Conflict increased around changes in liturgy and program planning. Some people left the church for "more traditional" congregations. One member accused Pastor Smith and the ministry team of undermining family values. They were "changing the whole church to make sure divorced people are included." At the end of the year, however, the team's evaluation was positive. Transformation in certain areas of congregational life seemed to have taken place. The Willis family had found a place of care. Though stepfamily life continued to be difficult for them, they had weathered their crisis and now had a supportive community.

In its final meeting, the forum and ministry team considered next steps. Jim pointed out that the forum's focus had been entirely internal. They were concerned with the "communion of saints," but divorced and remarried families were also impacted by powerful social and political factors. Where, he wondered, was a public forum that could address justice issues for these families? He proposed that the church be a public space where critical dialogue could take place about stepfamilies. Their work had produced an environment where it was safe to talk about divorce and remarriage without fear of judgment or condescension. Stepfamilies and others could tell their stories without further pillage of redemption's hope from well-meaning but poorly understanding folk. Shouldn't the church also interpret the gospel in a cultural context? This step toward justice, he believed, was now required.

Since the congregation had little experience as a "public forum," this idea became part of the ministry team's agenda for the next year. The forum, ministry team, and other interested church members watched for opportunities for community interaction. This resulted in one television conversation between Pastor Smith and a local politician who proposed "family values" legislation that excluded divorced and remarried families. Several church members launched a countercampaign, which articulated the congregation's inclusive values. One of Pastor Smith's colleagues agreed to write a weekly newspaper column about families in culture. The series promoted ideas of transformation and was controversial enough to spark an editorial debate in letters to the paper's religion editor. The church became known for work with divorced and remarried families, and leaders were asked to take part in corporate and community discussions about single-parent families and stepfamilies.

At the end of year two, the ministry team could speak clearly of how praxis had impacted their church, community policy, and some areas of social justice. Subjugated stepfamily stories, liberated by Christ's destabilizing gospel, were now part of the church's new redemptive narrative as well as an influence for love and justice in the larger community.

Chapter 9

Agenda:
Toward a Theological Vision
for Stepfamilies

Praxis, hermeneutical circulation, and creative theological imagining are processes of theological construction. They drive dialogical meaning-making and direct pastoral action. This constructive process happens in the community of faith. When applied to stepfamily experience, this action-reflection revises theological understandings of remarried couples and their families. A thoughtful theological rethinking of stepfamilies can articulate a vision that includes them as an integral part of a larger whole of redeemed humanity that constitutes the community of faith. Stepfamilies have special meaning. They are a particular people who share common themes in their story of redemption. They need care, but they also bring with them unique insight, which adds wisdom to the life of the church. By including stepfamily stories in the narrative of faith, our vision of God is broadened. We find new ways God is active in divorced and remarried families, and we see new dimensions of God's image revealed in stepfamilies made whole.

Whenever the church is asked to include those who are different, the community of faith experiences tension, which presses it into a reflective cycle. This is as old as Peter and Paul's conflict over inclusion of the Gentiles in Acts 15. In such cases, constructive theology reconsiders the nature of redemption and inclusion for people living in particular circumstances. We must make sense of strangers included—on what grounds does inclusion take place? How does inclusion affect our understanding of divorced and

173

remarried people, God, and community life? What does inclusion require of those who would be included? What does it require of the church? These questions are central to the church's self-reflective process in praxis, hermeneutical circulation, and creative theological imagining. The vision that unfolds from this process directs the church's ministry with stepfamilies. It also guides stepfamilies toward redemptive wholeness and full presence at Christ's table.

Several inchoate theological themes can guide a beginning theology for stepfamily ministry. These are rooted in foundational stepfamily experience and must be refined by future praxis and critical dialogue with stepfamilies in communities of faith.

Theme one: Divorced and remarried families are anchored in the soil of lost and broken promises. Sin and forgiveness are central to stepfamily care, inclusion, and call to community.

An adequate theological vision for stepfamilies turns to God's forgiveness and atonement. It is this gift that breaks divorced persons' debilitating captivity to guilt, shame, and self-recrimination in recycling grief. Baptism is a metaphor for God, who breaks in from beyond our past and empowers our transformation. In response, we turn from sinful acts and destructive relational patterns. We turn also to defiance and resist the influence of sinful cultural systems of power that have shaped us. Baptism is a regenerative vision that cycles through the Christian life. It calls believers to remember God's redeeming love, which cleanses us. It reminds us of our obligation to respond to that love. Baptism symbolizes God's grace and summons the baptized to faithfulness and discipleship.

A vision for stepfamilies includes a call to renewed baptismal vows. This does not mean rebaptism but a revitalized commitment by divorced persons to be available to God's empowering forgiveness, atonement, and call to transformed family living. It is this transformation that will compel divorced people to honor commitments to wounded children and draw them to resolve remnants of broken promises from past marriage. This transformation also grounds new promises in a community of faith that can resist those emotional and cultural powers that deceive and destroy. Baptism is the story of a renewed humanity departing on a path different from the past.

Congregations must reinterpret and refine the meaning of baptism as an inclusive regenerative metaphor that impacts divorced and remarried people in specific and concrete ways. Liturgies that reaffirm the baptismal covenant[1] provide a creative intersection where congregations and

---

[1]Presbyterian Church (U.S.A.), *Book of Common Worship* (Louisville: Westminster/John Knox Press, 1993).

remarrying couples can explore forgiveness and baptism as an ethical call to renewed lifestyles in remarriage. It is the church's mission to interpret God's redemptive activity to divorced and remarrying people and then provide a context of accountability that supports transformed living.

Theme two: Divorced and remarried families are anchored in the suffering of tragic loss and loss of faith in promise, which transcends the result of individual sin. Redemption for divorced and remarried families includes God's compassionate love, which stands with and chooses those who suffer.

There are many factors in divorce and remarriage that are beyond individual choice and control. These elevate grief and loss to suffering. Children's pain, partners who are abandoned or abused, destructive cultural powers that erode marital commitments, cultural marginalization of the divorced, and religious disenfranchisement provide a context that is tragic. In divorced families, tragedy results in loss of faith in promise and a spirit-killing relational malaise that robs a redeemed future. These transcend forgiveness and atonement. A vision for divorced and remarried families must include God's compassionate presence in brokenness that cannot be repaired.

Communion provides a metaphor of God's committed presence with suffering. God's compassionate love, embodied in the shared bread and cup of Christ's broken humanity, contains the helpless rage and sorrowing paralysis of tragic loss. Communion also symbolizes God's promise to act in tragic loss. Because of tragic loss, God's defiance of evil and its destructive power erupted into human history through Christ's resurrection. Out of the tomb of tragedy, God resurrected Christ and the faithful community. Communion symbolizes God's promise of compassionate presence and resurrected life through the community that shares suffering. Common union with Christ's death and resurrection empowers the faithful community to stand fast with suffering and preach a gospel of defiant hope against that which would rob the human spirit of its identity and vitality.

A vision for divorced and remarried people includes an image of God as one who relates to a torn world through compassionate love. God attends to concrete suffering and sorrow in ways that are appropriate to the situation. It is God's power to "suffer with" broken, divorced people that enlivens redemption. God's compassion, embodied in the faithful community, immerses itself in tragedy in order to struggle against it with those who suffer. This is incarnate in a relationship of solidarity between congregations and stepfamilies that can hold suffering people through sorrowing paralysis, and then name the evils against which divorced and remarried families struggle. This relationship hears a cry of helpless rage and then acts to transform it into empowered opposition to the political, social, judicial, and emotional forces that break hearts and bind remarried families' spirits.

Stepfamilies are broken by tragedy and need communion with the broken body and spilled blood of Christ. Their hope of resurrection is embodied in new relationships. Through praxis and critical dialogue, divorced and remarried families must join those with whom they are in communion and together define these new relationships. For stepfamilies, God's compassionate love is embodied by a call to renewed community, tentative trust in the community's promise, and honesty about brokenness. At this intersection, communion calls a congregation to empathic response and empowers a dialogical relationship that names and confronts the powers that hold families in tragic bondage.

Theme three: Remarriage brings together couples who have lost their original "homeland" of covenant promise. Their homes and sustaining family symbols have been shattered, and they now live in an exile of psychological and social homelessness. Hope for remarrying couples resides in exile ended, a wilderness traversed, and homes rebuilt with new covenants, symbols, and sustaining stories of restoration.

Remarried couples can find hope in theological images of exiles who return home through the wilderness. God's forgiveness and compassion provide courage to set off across unknown, uncharted land in order to rebuild a family life left in rubble. Homes restored are not the same as the original and never will be. Remarriage covenants are not the same as first-marriage covenants. They are restoration covenants that continuously call to mind gratitude that God has restored. Remarriage covenants do not deny or disown the past. Rather, they incorporate the past and its lament as part of an interpreted story that sets the stage for a new covenant future rooted in God's grace.

A theological vision for remarrying couples requires an ethic of reconstruction. Remarriage is a harder, more complex, and more dangerous covenant than first marriage. It must be a response to a vocational call to rebuild something new out of old wreckage. This requires preparation, commitment, faithfulness, and diligent hard work with little immediate payoff. The old rubble of past destructive relational patterns, oppressive guilt, and denial of responsibility for marital failure must be cleared away. In its place, remarried couples must work hard to construct solid foundations and strong family walls that will withstand challenges from inside and out. The end product will look very different from the original. Hope is found not in replicating an old city and its houses but in joy that springs from constructing something new.

An exile and restoration metaphor gives direction to the church's response to remarrying couples. Its first task is to find, identify, and name God's restoring activity among those who are divorced and remarrying. Together with remarrying couples, the church must interpret the vocation of remarriage and its meaning in the life of the church. As a faithful community, the church is also responsible for prophetic proclamation, which articulates this vocational vision. It must ask remarrying couples for accountability and then participate in opposing social and legal systems that undermine stepfamily growth. Part of its work must be to help divorced and remarrying couples evaluate their call as rebuilders and then help them prepare for the harsh realities that await their hope and vocational commitment.

The church cannot be a neutral bystander wondering if returned exiles will actually "pull it off." Neither can it be one of the hecklers on the hillside who discourage reconstruction and fail to see God's redemptive work in motion. Congregations and remarrying couples must find a point of unity in their mutual baptism and communion that allows each to fulfill their part of the restoration covenant.

Theme four: Remarried families are an embodiment of hope that relies on and incarnates God's inclusive, impartial love.

Perhaps here lies the clearest moral vision for stepfamilies. Couples are called to a vocation of restoration that is focused in commitment to children-who-are-not-mine. This will take priority over immediate marital satisfaction. Consequently, a call to remarriage is necessarily a call to parenting and stepparenting. Like remarriage, stepparenting is vocation. It requires self-transcendence and commitment to living out Christ's model of impartial love and justice. This must be done in a complex and volatile emotional field. As a developing moral vision, stepfamily vocation includes much of what Don Browning and his colleagues advocate in critical familism. Stepfamilies struggling toward wholeness will attend to gender equality, resistance of patriarchy, commitment to children's well-being, sanity in work commitments, and shared responsibility in the family. In addition, stepfamily as vocation asks remarried couples to live out an ethic of restoration that may require more effort and self-sacrifice than does Browning's critical familism.

This vision of remarried hope is grounded in God's impartial love, which was embodied in the life and death of Christ and then expressed again in the resurrection community. Like all moral visions, this ideal is possible only because of God's grace and only as it lives through the faithful community. It is a vision that will press the church to self-evaluation and transformation. The church must model and teach inclusive love that can support stepparents, who must set aside their own needs and respond to children who are not theirs. The community of faith must model for stepfamilies how to include step- kinds of people at a common table. Its example must show how justice inspires parents and children to share equally with those who only partially "belong."

This theological theme introduced into critical dialogue with stepfamilies holds great potential for constructive theological reflection. It may also be instructive for the church as stepfamilies express an expanded dimension of *imago dei* by living out God's impartial, inclusive love where it makes the least sense.

Together, these four themes provide a beginning place for congregational reflection and an emergent theology for stepfamilies. Discovering the fullness of stepfamily promise through reflective engagement with divorced and remarried families is the future theological task for the church.